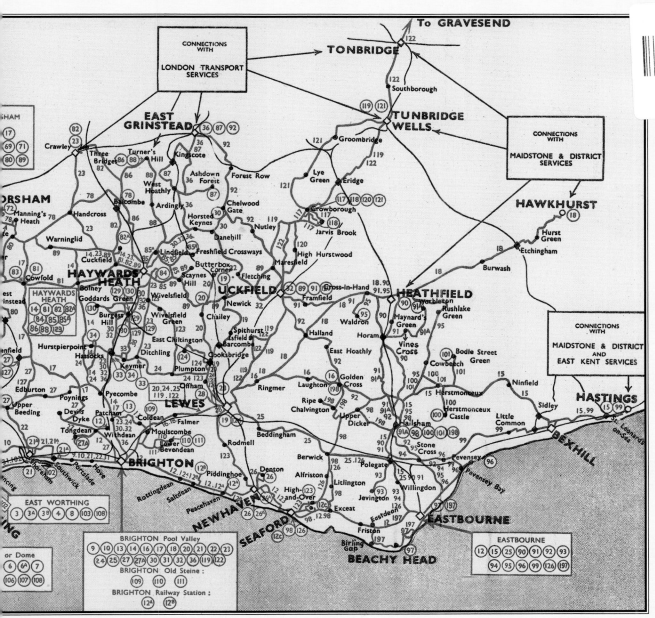

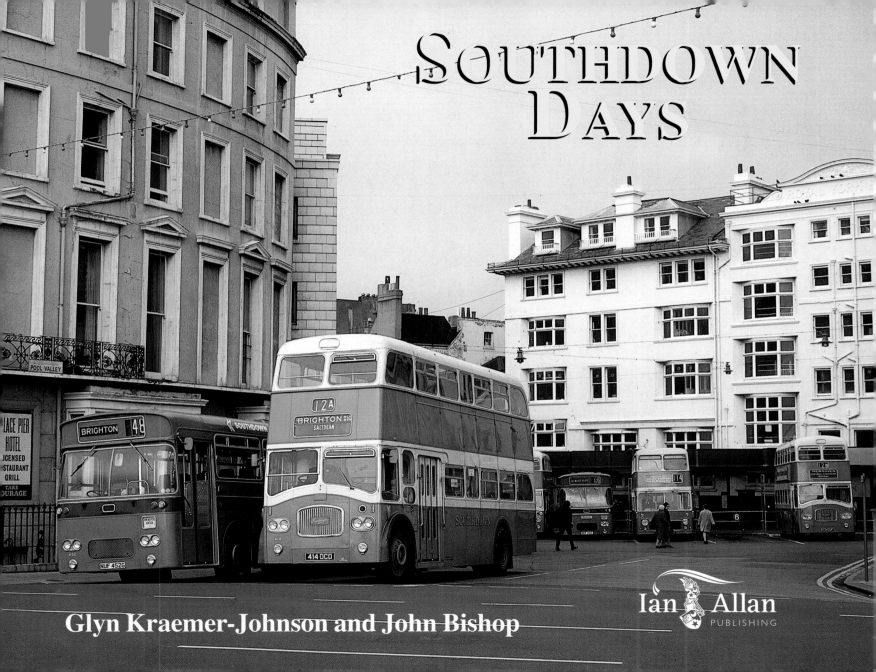

SOUTHDOWN DAYS

Glyn Kraemer-Johnson and John Bishop

Ian Allan PUBLISHING

Front cover: Some 65 miles long, route 122, linking Brighton with Gravesend, took just over four hours to complete. In places it was very rural, as is apparent from this view of East Lancs-bodied Leyland PD2/12 800 (RUF 200) heading south near Plaxtol, Kent, in 1969. The driver in his white cap looks well at ease despite the narrowness of the road. *Dave Brown*

Back cover: Some Sussex villages retain their character in the 21st century, one such being Findon, north of Worthing, but alas Guy Arab 417 (GUF 117) has long since been consigned to history. Route 2 took the main road, serving all the villages between Horsham and Worthing, but on this occasion (31 March 1963) 417 was on a Southdown Enthusiasts' Club tour. *Malcolm Keeping*

Title page: When this scene in Pool Valley was recorded in the early 1970s the most numerous Southdown double-decker was still the 'Queen Mary' Leyland PD3, three of which are visible here. Convertible 414 (414 DCD) of 1964 still shows 'Brighton' and would thus have come from the direction of Peacehaven. Standing alongside, with NBC-style fleetname, is a dual-purpose Northern Counties-bodied Leyland Leopard dating from 1969. Royal York Buildings survives today, but the main visitors to Pool Valley are National Express coaches. The sign on the left is dated, for with the sad demise of the West Pier the Palace Pier is now plain 'Brighton Pier'. *John Bishop*

CONTENTS

Narrative by Glyn Kraemer-Johnson
Photographs selected and captioned by John Bishop

First published 2005
ISBN (10) 0 7110 3077 4
ISBN (13) 978 0 7110 3077 0

Published by Ian Allan Publishing

an imprint of Ian Allan Publishing Ltd, Hersham, Surrey KT12 4RG

Printed in England by Ian Allan Printing Ltd, Hersham, Surrey KT12 4RG

Code: 0509/B2

Visit the Ian Allan Publishing website at www.ianallanpublishing.com

Left: Time was when Southdown had a large fleet of smart two-tone-green coaches, two of which are seen engaged on tour work in this July 1952 scene. On the left, prepared for a day trip to Brighton, is Beadle-bodied Leyland Tiger PS1 1298 (HUF 298) of 1949, while alongside, bound for Hayling Island, is Park Royal-bodied Leyland Cheetah LZ3 602 (EUF 502) dating from 1938. *J. Turley / Gordon Dinnage Transport Photographs*

INTRODUCTION

"If you spent as much time on your schoolwork as you do studying bus timetables, you'd do a lot better!" That was Mother from the kitchen. I disagreed with her then and I disagree now. I learned a lot from studying buses, especially timetables. I came to know Sussex in general and Brighton in particular like the back of my hand. I knew how to get anywhere in the Southdown area, even places to which I'd never been. By the age of 10 I knew a great many of the pubs in Sussex and Hampshire. After all, 'Chailey, King's Head', 'Findon, Gun Inn' and 'Pyecombe, The Plough' tripped off the tongue as though the three words were one. I learned that South Parade Pier was in Southsea and that, like Brighton, Worthing had a Dome. I remember being quite disappointed when I discovered it was only a cinema and not a Royal Palace!

From this knowledge came an interest in local history, which was heightened by taking half-day coach excursions and listening to the descriptions of places of interest given by the drivers, although this often conflicted with what had been said by a previous driver, and much of it proved to be mythical. Nevertheless I learned a lot.

Moreover I learned something that so many people today are quite unable to do; I learned to read a timetable! No, Mother, I still disagree that my education suffered because of my interest in buses. Mind you, there were the times when I would play truant from school that you never knew about. Not for me the pictures or amusement arcades. I would take myself off for a bus ride. Usually they were comparatively short, to Eastbourne maybe, or Worthing. On other occasions I would make a marathon day trip to Portsmouth or Gravesend. In the case of the latter I would sometimes make it into a round-trip, travelling from Gravesend to London by Green Line and returning to Brighton by Southdown express. These marathons, it must be admitted, were generally taken legally during the school holidays, as it was impossible to make such a trip and return home by normal school finishing time.

As well as visiting places that had hitherto been no more than names in a timetable, my outings gave me the chance to see some of the rarer Southdown vehicles — types that were rarely if ever seen in Brighton, such as the Leyland PD2 double-deck coach, Dennis Falcons and Bedford OBs. They also brought me into contact with neighbouring operators, such as Provincial, Aldershot & District and East Kent.

In contrast with many other parts of the country, independent operators in the South East were few and far between, but there were some that ran fascinating rarities I was ever anxious to see. Then there were the operators that ran wholly within the Southdown area, such as Brighton, Hove & District, Hastings Tramways and the corporations of Brighton, Eastbourne and Portsmouth. Oh, if only I'd had a camera back then!

Such trips as these form the basis of this book. Starting from Brighton, we travel by various services to the boundaries of the Southdown area, looking at the vehicles seen *en route*, both of Southdown and of other operators, and, at the various termini, the buses of those companies whose areas adjoined Southdown territory. Several circular trips could be made: from Brighton to Eastbourne on service 25 via Lewes, returning by the coast road, or to East Grinstead on service 36, returning by the 92 to Uckfield and the 119 or 122 thence to Brighton. And most of these services were operated by double-deckers, so one could sit back in those comfortably shaped seats and enjoy a marvellous view of the rolling Sussex countryside.

Then there were the legitimate school outings. The only one I remember from infant school was to Hassocks on a lowbridge utility Guy. What a bonus! Later came trips to the British Museum and (far more interesting) the Science Museum on a Duple-bodied Leyland Royal Tiger, to St Albans on a Beadle rebuild and to the Roman villa at Bignor on a Gurney Nutting-bodied Bedford belonging to Alpha Coaches of Brighton.

To produce a book about Southdown and its fellow operators, does one stick rigidly to a particular time, describing what would have been seen in the 'Fifties alone and ignoring what came before and after? Or should one take a broader canvas, describing the scene without being confined to a particular period? We have opted for a middle course,

Above: Whilst all-Leyland Titan PD2/12 720 (KUF 720) takes centre stage in this scene in the Old Steine, Brighton, on route 9, there is much of interest in the background. Although the view is undated, the presence on the far right of an apparently brand-new convertible-open-top 'Queen Mary' Leyland PD3 would seem to date the picture to the spring of 1964.
On the left a Brighton, Hove & District convertible Bristol Lodekka is partially obscuring a handsome Brighton Corporation AEC Regent, whilst further back is one of the first BH&D Lodekkas, with Cave-Brown-Cave heating/ventilation system.
Malcolm Keeping

selecting the 25 years following the end of World War 2. Thus, whilst in reality the journeys described were taken mainly in the late 'Fifties, we have included what might have been seen on earlier or later visits. Some artistic licence has been used, for there are instances of vehicles' being described which could not have been seen together. Similarly routes and services were changed throughout the period, and mention may be made of a journey or connection that could have been made only at certain times during our chosen period.

This was a particularly fascinating time for the bus industry. In 1945 most operators were struggling to cope with prewar vehicles, many long past their sell-by date, vehicle shortages brought about by requisitioned and war-damaged buses and a fleet that was suffering from a lack of proper maintenance. True, there had been new vehicles delivered during the war, but these were non-standard and built from poor-quality materials. Southdown itself had received some 100 Guy Arabs, and it has to be said that they probably proved to be a lot more rugged and reliable than was expected, leading to further orders for the type in peacetime.

The late 'Forties and early 'Fifties saw extensive rebodying and rebuilding programmes of prewar and wartime vehicles, and such

buses would form the backbone of the Southdown fleet for many years to come. New buses and coaches were purchased as quickly as they could be built, and many new bodybuilders appeared on the scene. Firms previously engaged in building high-class cars or even aircraft suddenly saw a huge new market in building bus and, particularly, coach bodies. The early 'Fifties also saw the introduction of the Bristol Lodekka, a low-frame chassis with a dropped-centre rear axle that enabled the fitting of a normal body with central gangways on both decks whilst still maintaining a low overall height. The Lodekka and its imitators brought about the demise of the old 'lowbridge' double-deckers, with awkward sunken offside gangway on the upper deck.

This was truly the heyday of British bus travel, a time when passenger numbers were reaching their peak, before the popularity of the motor car and television began to bring about a decline. When this began it was countered by the introduction of one-man operation, initially on single-deckers but extended in the 'Sixties to double-deckers; it also led to the purchase of buses with sparsely finished lightweight bodies, in an effort to reduce fuel consumption, but this was something of which Southdown could never be accused.

With the introduction of larger vehicles and one-man operation the front entrance became the norm, and in 1958 appeared the first rear-engined double-decker, in the shape of the Leyland Atlantean. Maidstone & District (from 1959) and Portsmouth (1962) were early users of the type, but operators in the South East were virtually unanimous in remaining faithful to the front-engined double-decker until they were left with no alternative. At the end of our period came the birth of the National Bus Company, which robbed operators of their individuality and submerged their identities beneath a sea of leaf-green or poppy-red paint. It was indeed a fascinating time.

Only when John and I began to research this book did we realise just how vast the subject was, and within the confines of this volume we have been able only to scratch the surface. It has certainly not been possible to include, either pictorially or in words, every type of vehicle that operated in the region during what amounts to a quarter of a century. Nor has it been possible to describe in depth operators such as Hants & Sussex or Dengate's of Rye, whose fascinating fleets and history could (and have) filled books on their own. We have not listed vehicle numbers or gone into great detail about their specification; this is not that kind of book. What we have tried to do is to present a balanced picture of an area and a period of which we have fond memories, and we hope that the following pages will enable you to share them.

Glyn Kraemer-Johnson
Hailsham, East Sussex
September 2005

Above: Southdown's coaching fleet was widely admired and was synonymous with quality and reliability. Seen in June 1973 awaiting passengers for a day out from one of the hotels in First Avenue, Hove, car 1730 (8730 CD) was a 1961 Leyland Leopard L2 / Harrington Cavalier, which combination for many represented the zenith of coach design. Alas Thomas Harrington's Sackville Works in Hove is long gone, and Leyland Motors is now also but a memory. *John Bishop*

Far right: Many photographs are taken in Brighton's Pool Valley bus station, but very few at its entrance in the Old Steine, as here. This early-1960s shot was taken to record the use of the rear destination display, which would soon be overpainted. Seen on a cold Sunday in winter, Northern Counties-bodied Leyland PD3/5 949 (6949 CD) of 1961 arrives at the end of the long route 31 from Southsea, which journey would have taken nearly four hours. Note (on the left) the discreet 'Southdown' sign; also the classic British cars of the period. *John Bishop*

Right: Apparently brand-new, Leyland Titan PD3/Northern Counties 891 (2891 CD) of 1961 stands in Brighton's Pool Valley bus station, prior to departing on a short working of the 'main road' route 31. Advertising for Clark's Bread was for many years a typical feature of buses in Brighton. *D. Clark / Southdown Enthusiasts' Club*

Service 31, running between Brighton and Southsea with a weekday frequency of 15 minutes, was Southdown's prestige route, usually receiving the newest vehicles. That said, it was very much a Leyland stronghold, and only rarely was a Guy to be seen at work on the service. Even in the days of the National Bus Company, when the Bristol VR reigned supreme, the service (by then numbered 700) was operated for some time by Leyland Atlanteans.

In the late 'Forties, following a brief period of operation by Leyland PD1s, the service received an allocation of brand new all-Leyland PD2/1s. These were replaced by successive batches of PD2/12s with bodies by various builders until the beginning of the 'Sixties, when the

ubiquitous Northern Counties-bodied PD3s took over. Interestingly the first of these 'Queen Marys' (as they were to become known) were not allocated to the 31, but more of that later.

At the time of my schoolboy journeys the Leyland PD2/12 was the usual fare. Most common were those with Leyland's own 'Farington' bodywork — handsome buses by any standard, and which in Southdown's case were given some individuality by having winding half-drop windows rather than the usual sliding vents. They were later joined by the more ungainly Northern Counties-bodied version, which somehow contrived to look about 10ft wide when viewed from the rear; in view of what was to follow, it was strange that of 112 PD2/12s (excluding the coach) only 10 were bodied by Northern Counties. Next came the Park Royal variant, still with half-drop windows. These were largely replaced in 1956/7, when Southdown took delivery of a further 36 PD2/12s, 12 bodied by Beadle to Park Royal design and 24 by East Lancs. And what superb buses these were, epitomising what must surely have been the zenith of British bus design.

Strange are the things that stick in the mind. A lasting memory of all these PD2s is of the heaters. On the upper deck this was situated under the front nearside seat, so the place to sit was in the second seat from the front, where one's feet could rest against the heater outlet. They were pretty pathetic things that would whirr into life when the bus began to move and would die completely when it came to rest. On cold days one could only hope that stops would not be too lengthy.

Like all of Southdown's out-of-town services, the 31 departed from Brighton's Pool Valley bus station, turning west along the seafront and passing, on the right, the town's most prestigious hotels and, on the left, the West Pier, which sadly is no more. The route paralleled Brighton, Hove & District's famous open-top service 17 as far as Portslade; this service, started

Right: At Worthing the Southdown route 31 would meet with town services, which in the early postwar years were operated mainly by the wartime utility Guy Arabs. The first of these, delivered in 1943, was 400 (GCD 974), although by the time this photograph was taken its original Northern Counties body had been replaced by a 1945 East Lancs version first mounted on a prewar Leyland TD2. Route 7 operated between Lancing and Worthing Pier, where all the local routes converged.
D. Clark / Southdown Enthusiasts' Club

in 1936 with a fleet of Tilling ST-type AEC Regents fitted with new purpose-built open-top bodywork by ECW, must surely have been one of the first instances (if not *the* first) of specially built open-top vehicles operating on a service aimed specifically at holidaymakers and day-trippers. The Regents were replaced in the early 'Fifties by prewar Bristol K5Gs rebuilt to convertible open-top in BH&D's workshops, and these in turn gave way to Bristol Lodekkas also with detachable tops. Open-top buses in the BH&D fleet wore a smart livery of cream with black bonnet and wings and, in the early days, black lining-out, and they were always treated to a 'touch-up and varnish' (if not a complete repaint) at the beginning of each season.

Joining the seafront at West Street and also running as far as Portslade was BH&D service 8, a circular service operating from Portslade via Hangleton and the Old Shoreham Road to Brighton

station, running thence via West Street and the seafront back to Portslade. A lightly trafficked route, this was worked mainly by older vehicles cascaded from front-line services. In the late 'Forties and early 'Fifties the route had been worked mainly by Tilling ST-type AECs dating from the early 'Thirties that had been either rebodied by ECW or Beadle or rebuilt by BH&D. These were replaced by standard Bristol/ECW K5Gs and KS5Gs, these latter having 7ft 6in-wide chassis with 8ft-wide bodies. This all changed in 1968, when the service was equipped with brand-new Bristol REs and became BH&D's first one-man-operated route, at least in modern times, the REs later being replaced by the company's first Bristol VRs.

At Portslade BH&D's services left the seafront and would not be seen again (at least not until 1961, when under the Brighton Area Transport Services agreement the boundary was extended to Shoreham

Beach and red-and-cream Bristols could be encountered again in Shoreham High Street). The 31 followed the coast road through Fishersgate and Southwick, passed the power station, timber yards and coal wharves lining Shoreham Harbour, crossed the impressive Norfolk Bridge and carried on through Lancing to Worthing (Dome!).

From Worthing, as well as the 9, 10 and 31 coastal services there were two trunk routes operating inland, service 1 to Pulborough and service 2 to Horsham, both of which in the late 'Fifties were worked largely by Park Royal-bodied Guy Arab IVs. For many years Worthing's town services had been operated mainly by utility Guys, including those that had originally been lowbridge and had been

Left: Pictured at Worthing Pier in the early 1960s, just before the demise of the last covered-top utility Guy Arabs, is Northern Counties-bodied 458 (GUF 158) on route 5 to Findon, just north of Worthing. Worthing was the last stronghold for the type, the last running in May 1963; open-top conversions continued until replaced the following year by new convertible 'Queen Marys'.
John Bishop

Left: Delivered in 1961/2, the 40 Northern Counties-bodied Leyland PD3/5s, with pneumocyclic semi-automatic transmission in lieu of the manual epicyclic type, did not perform well on hills and thus tended to gravitate to the flatter parts of the Southdown empire, notably Portsmouth and Worthing. Seen at Worthing Pier in August 1967, 947 (6947 CD) awaits passengers on local route 17; behind is 671 (271 AUF), a Marshall-bodied Leyland Leopard new in 1963 and one of 30 which would be transferred to East Kent in 1971.
Southdown Enthusiasts' Club

9

Right: A truly nostalgic scene at Worthing, where routes either radiated out into the countryside or, like the fondly remembered 31 from Brighton to Southsea, would pass through along the coast. Departing on a relief working of service 2, 745 (MCD 745), an all-Leyland PD2/12 dating from 1953, will make its way north up the main A24 London road towards Horsham. Behind, East Lancs-bodied Leyland Royal Tiger 1508 (LUF 508) awaits passengers on a local town route. The photograph dates from 1966, at which time *Batman* was showing at the Dome cinema. *John Bishop*

rebodied with highbridge East Lancs bodies taken from Leyland TDs, these rarely seeming to appear elsewhere in the Southdown area. All-Leyland PD2/1s took over in the early 'Sixties, to be followed by Guy Arab IVs when these were displaced from front-line services. The town also received a number of the PD3/5 'Queen Marys' with pneumocyclic gearboxes, these being more at home on Worthing's flat terrain.

In prewar days Worthing had been home to the Tramocar operation, which had used small-wheeled Shelvoke & Drewry Freighters on a seafront service. The company was taken over by Southdown in 1938, whereafter the Freighters were replaced by Dennis Falcons with centre-entrance Harrington bodywork; these could still be seen in the town until 1950, when they were moved to Hayling Island.

The West Sussex coastal plain is flat and fairly uninteresting, and in the author's opinion the journey from Worthing to Chichester was quite boring. A highlight, at Bognor Regis bus station, would be a glimpse of the two ECW-bodied Leyland PS1s in use as Left Luggage offices and, perhaps, car 700, the unique Leyland PD2/12 double-deck coach that ended its days somewhat ignominiously working school services in the area. Also operating into Bognor was Aldershot & District, with a service from Midhurst via Chichester which always seemed a little out of place in the heart of Southdown territory.

Chichester, with its Market Cross and imposing cathedral, offered more of interest, especially the bus station, which was usually a hive of activity, offering a wide spectrum of buses and coaches typifying the Southdown fleet. As well as double- and single-deck buses there would be Southdown coaches on express and excursion work, together with the Dennis Lancets and AEC Reliances of East Kent and Bristols of Royal Blue passing through on the South Coast Express service from Margate to Bournemouth and beyond.

And so over the county boundary into Hampshire. At Emsworth would be found the first independent operator to be encountered since leaving Brighton. This was Southern Motorways, one of the many incarnations of Hants & Sussex Motor Services, operated by entrepreneur Basil Williams, and using a version of its attractive two-tone red and cream livery. In the late 'Sixties the company operated a fleet of half a dozen ex-London Transport GS-class Guy Specials, these being the mainstay of the service to Thorney Island which Hants & Sussex had started back in 1939. There were, however, many other gems in the fleet, including an ex-United Counties rebodied Bristol JO5G and two Willowbrook-bodied Guy Arab LUF coaches that had originated with Black & White Motorways.

Hants & Sussex is a name that crops up repeatedly in this book. It operated in pockets throughout Sussex, Hampshire and Surrey, including Winchester, Fareham, Emsworth, Midhurst, Horsham and Crawley. The story of Hants & Sussex, its subsidiaries and various incarnations is a fascinating one but too involved to go into here. Interested readers are referred to the history of the company by Alan Lambert published in 1982, which is still available from the author.

Above: Bognor Regis was the final home of car 700 (KUF 700), the unique Northern Counties-bodied Leyland PD2 delivered in 1950. Coach-seated, with full front and toplights above the side windows, this was a grand vehicle but alas overweight and ended its days downgraded to bus work, surviving until 1966. Coincidentally route 31 to Southsea, for which this vehicle would have been well suited, later adopted the number 700, but by that time KUF 700 was but a memory. *Southdown Enthusiasts' Club*

Right: Before the relief road past the market at Chichester was made suitable for all vehicles buses would make their way to/from the bus station via the city's mediæval market cross, allowing enthusiasts the opportunity to take photographs such as this of Northern Counties-bodied Leyland Titan PD3/5 937 (6937 CD) turning into West Street *en route* for Portsmouth and Southsea. *Peter Trevaskis*

In the early 1970s Southdown Motor Services was a proud company with an enviable reputation enhanced by its buildings, exemplified by Bognor Regis bus station. As well as being the terminus for local routes such as the 51A, upon which Marshall-bodied Bristol RESL 487 (TCD 487J) is pictured, this would play host to Aldershot & District vehicles from Surrey as well as Southdown double-deckers passing through on the famous 31 between Brighton and Southsea.
John Bishop

Right: The setting for this nearside view of 1512 (MCD 512) is Chichester garage, which along with the bus station was built in the late 1950s. A Leyland Royal Tiger with East Lancs bodywork, this bus was built with centre entrance (located where the fleetname is seen here) and in common with all of its type was rebuilt in the 1958-61 period. The 54 was very much a rural route, passing through settlements with suitably rural Sussex names, which linked Chichester with Petersfield. Chichester bus station is today the registered office of Southdown Motor Services, which trades variously as Stagecoach Coastline, Stagecoach in Portsmouth and Stagecoach in the South Downs. *Malcolm Keeping*

Havant, a couple of miles further on, was another interesting 'junction'. From here services ran to Hayling Island, and for many years a weak bridge precluded the use of all but the lightest of vehicles. Even then passengers had to alight and follow the bus across the bridge on foot! Dennis Falcons were the usual fare, 10 with lightweight 30-seat bodies by Dennis having been purchased in 1949 specifically for the job. They were joined by the two 1939 Harrington-bodied examples from the former Tramocar operation in Worthing. Also used on the Hayling services, again because of their light weight, were survivors from the fleet of Leyland Cubs, one of which had its seats removed and operated a shuttle service across the bridge. Other vehicles purchased especially for Hayling Island services were most unusual for Southdown, being standard Duple-bodied Bedford OBs (albeit with seating capacity reduced to 27 from the usual 29) bought to assist elderly Leyland Cheetahs on express services to and from the island. However, in 1958 a new bridge was opened, eliminating the need for special vehicles.

The next point of interest was Farlington, where one would get one's first glimpse of buses in the splendid crimson and white livery of Portsmouth Corporation — or, to use its correct and more grandiose title, the City of Portsmouth Passenger Transport Department.

Above: Travelling on the 31 through Havant one could observe the small single-deckers used on route 47, which crossed the coast road on its way between the station and Hayling Island. All were lightweight buses, on account of the frail bridge connecting the island with the mainland. Seen loading for Havant at Beachlands *c*1952 is 91 (JUF 91), an all-Dennis Falcon new in 1949. Note the conductor in smart summer Southdown uniform complete with white hat; also the informative bus stops. *The Omnibus Society*

Left: With journey's end almost in sight, passengers on route 31 to Portsmouth would catch their first glimpse of Portsmouth Corporation buses on the A27 outside the city limits. These would be Leylands, smartly turned out in maroon and white, exemplified by 111 (ORV 988), a 1958 PD2/40 with Metro-Cammell Orion body, albeit seen here at the Dockyard terminus in Portsmouth. Route 148B was one of a group of services serving Leigh Park, a large overspill estate outside the Portsmouth city boundary. *V. C. Jones / Southdown Enthusiasts' Club*

15

2. PASSING THROUGH POMPEY

Right: Portsmouth continued to favour Metro-Cammell bodywork in the 1960s, by now on rear-engined Leyland Atlantean chassis. Pictured when newly into service in 1963, 220 (220 BTP) shows how an uninspiring design can be enhanced by a superb livery with lining-out. Service 143B operated past the airport, thereafter joining Southdown routes for a short way before going to Leigh Park, Havant. The airport has now disappeared under housing and industrial development. *V. C. Jones / Southdown Enthusiasts' Club*

Far right: When the Metro-Cammell Orion body was introduced in the mid-1950s on the Leyland Titan PD2/12 chassis it was considered by enthusiasts to be a case of 'back to basics'. Compared with contemporary Southdown deliveries Portsmouth's examples were indeed basic, but their handsome lined-out livery contrived to improve their appearance. No 88 (LRV 980) of 1956 stands by a typically informative bus stop at Canoe Lake, near South Parade Pier, Southsea, in July 1971. *Dave Brown*

A co-ordination scheme between Portsmouth Corporation and Southdown came into effect in July 1946 — some 15 years before a similar agreement was reached in Brighton — and brought about the co-ordination of all services in an area bounded by Fareham in the west, Petersfield to the north and Emsworth in the east. Although Corporation buses rarely ran as far as the area boundaries, the CPPTD was able to introduce services operating well beyond the city limits, into what had previously been solely Southdown territory. The crimson-and-white buses thus reached such places as Paulsgrove and Portchester in the west and, in the east, the growing satellite town of Leigh Park, where, unusually, the depot was shared by the two operators.

The buses most commonly seen on the 148 group of services to Farlington and Leigh Park were initially the Corporation's Weymann Orion-bodied Leyland PD2/12s. These must have been amongst the oddest Orions ever built. They had the typical unequal-depth windows on upper

and lower decks, and the front and rear domes — frameless and with flush-fitting windows — were pure Orion, but the side windows were inset, square-cornered and of the half-drop variety. The PD2s were subsequently joined by a batch of PD3s, again with Weymann bodywork, but to the standard Orion design. The body style, always somewhat ungainly, was helped considerably by the Corporation's superb livery of crimson with white window surrounds, grey roof and gold lining-out. Next came Atlanteans, Portsmouth being an early user of the type. These too had the standard Weymann body, and again the appearance was helped immensely by the livery, even though the grey roofs had by this time been abandoned.

Having passed through Farlington the 31 crossed onto Portsea Island and made for Hilsea, where a stop outside the large Southdown garage invariably revealed something of interest. By and large the Southdown buses working in the Portsmouth area were similar to those to be found elsewhere, but there were exceptions. The 12 Northern Counties-bodied Guy Arab IIIs of 1948 were split between Portsmouth and Brighton and were rarely seen elsewhere, so it was always interesting to track down those that were 'missing' from the Brighton allocation. In later years one looked out for the original Brighton, Hove & District Bristol VRs, which were transferred to Portsmouth following the Southdown takeover of BH&D.

Right: Southdown's principal garage in Portsmouth was located at Hilsea. Prior to the opening of the M275 motorway the road at this point was one of only two main routes onto Portsea Island, and consequently the duplication by Southdown of Portsmouth Corporation routes was unavoidable. Seen outside the Southdown garage in the early 1950s is Portsmouth 194 (DRV 108), a Weymann-bodied Leyland Titan PD1 of 1948; note the maroon-painted radiator surround. *W. J. Haynes / Southdown Enthusiasts' Club*

Right: Every enthusiast likes to peer into depots, wondering which vehicles are 'resting'. Such was the case in the early 1960s at Hilsea, where a young Bishop discovered a visiting Western National Bristol LS coach sharing accommodation with two prewar Leyland TD5 Titans rebodied postwar by Park Royal, 223 (FUF 223) and 258 (GCD 358), and a Northern Counties-bodied utility Guy Arab, 438 (GUF 138). Note the Southdown practice of placing the registration number between decks, even though there is provision below the radiator grille; also the embossed radiator badge proclaiming '*Southdown*' instead of '**LEYLAND**'. *John Bishop*

Above: Southdown's main garage in the Portsmouth area was located at Hilsea, near Cosham, in the north of the city. Outside peak hours one could find various vehicles that were otherwise difficult to photograph or (as here) a combination of liveries. On the left of the picture is Leyland PD3/4 311 (FCD 311D), freshly repainted in NBC livery, whilst taking centre stage is ex-Brighton, Hove & District Bristol VR 2099 (OCD 769G), now in apple green and cream but with NBC-style fleetname and grey wheels. On the right, still in full Southdown livery, is Northern Counties-bodied PD3/5 934 (6934 CD) with pneumocyclic semi-automatic gearbox in place of the standard epicyclic manual transmission; new in 1961/2, the 40 buses of this batch were to prove less than popular, and subsequent deliveries reverted to the manual type. *John Bishop*

Portsmouth Corporation originally had a rather idiosyncratic route-numbering system. Trolleybus routes were allocated numbers, while motor-bus routes were given letters. Moreover, different letters or numbers were given depending upon the direction of travel; thus the trolleybus route from Green Lane to the Dockyard was numbered 11, whereas journeys in the reverse direction were 12s.

The trolleybus fleet consisted of two main types — Cravens-bodied AEC 661Ts dating back to the mid-'Thirties and curvaceous Burlingham-bodied BUTs delivered in 1950/1. Personal memories are

of the Cravens-bodied AECs, with plush seating and lots of dark, creaking woodwork.

As far as the motor-bus fleet was concerned Portsmouth was a Leyland stronghold, from the TD4 through to the Atlantean (including unusual single-deck versions with Seddon coachwork) and the Leyland National. There were some diversions, however, particularly during World War 2, when a number of Bedford OWB single-deckers and Daimler double-deckers were taken into stock. In the early postwar years two batches of Crossley double-deckers were purchased, the first

being bodied by local coachbuilder Reading, the second having Crossley's own distinctive bodywork. The all-Crossleys had an early form of automatic gearbox and were known as 'gearless'; riding on them was quite an odd experience. They were not successful, however, and were subsequently given engines and gearboxes from withdrawn Leyland TD4s.

And so, after four hours, the 31 arrived at South Parade Pier, its western terminus. Southdown is generally thought of as a Sussex company, but it actually operated well into Hampshire. By the time

the 31 arrived at its final destination it was some 11 miles inside the county boundary, and there was still a fair way to go to the borders of the company's territory.

Although Southdown usually allocated its newest vehicles to the prestige 12 or 31 services, there was one memorable occasion when this did not happen. The buses in question were the very first Leyland PD3s, all of which were allocated to Portsmouth for service 45. This service started from Southsea, South Parade Pier, and, having passed through Portsmouth, turned westward to Fareham. The route was particularly

Left: Portsmouth Corporation's buses always looked smart in their livery of deep maroon and white with grey roof, as carried by 129 (RV 6370), an all-Leyland Titan TD5 of 1935, seen passing HMS *Vernon* as it approaches the Dockyard in the early 1960s. Note the trolleybus wires still *in situ. John Bishop*

Lower left: In 1962, when this photograph was taken, Portsmouth had much to keep the enthusiast happy, the municipal fleet comprising various types including 4 (DTP 813), a 1948 Leyland Titan PD1 with locally built Reading body, seen passing The Horseshoe public house, on the corner of Kings Road, Southsea, on its way to The Hard, then better known as the Dockyard. As was often the case with PD1s the radiator surround was painted — a practice not continued on the later PD2 model. *John Bishop*

Right: A photograph pre-dating the period covered by *Southdown Days* but which nevertheless affords a fine view of Southsea's South Parade Pier, journey's end for numerous Southdown routes in the Portsmouth area. Before the war the trams were very much in evidence; visible are three open-top cars (queuing) and (in the far distance) a covered-top car jostling with the ultimately all-conquering motor buses in fully lined-out Portsmouth livery. The pier itself is in original form, in which it would survive until ravaged by an horrendous fire in the 1970s. *John Bishop collection (photographer unknown)*

Right: With South Parade Pier in the background, Northern Counties-bodied Guy Arab III 507 (JCD 507) of 1948 bathes in the afternoon sun at Southsea before setting off westwards to Fareham on route 45; this would be a short working, for other journeys would travel on further, to Warsash. There is a distinctly holiday atmosphere, with deck chairs and ladies in sleeveless dresses strolling along the promenade, oblivious of the elegant lines of the bus and the livery which one day would be gone. *Eric Surfleet / Southdown Enthusiasts' Club*

interesting from an enthusiast's point of view, for at Fareham it met up with the emerald-green buses of the Gosport & Fareham Omnibus Co, otherwise known as Provincial.

During the 'Fifties and 'Sixties Provincial operated a fascinating selection of vehicles, which included some incredibly ancient AECs; as well as Regals dating from 1931 and 1934 that had been rebodied with full-front bodies there were Regent double-deckers dating from the mid- to late 'Thirties, some rebodied but others retaining their original Weymann or Park Royal bodywork. Other gems included a Brush-bodied Regent of 1932 and a utility Bristol K5G, both having been converted to open-top. However, the fleet was probably most famous for its Guy Arab double-deckers, a number of which had been fitted with Deutz air-cooled engines. A lasting impression of the

company was of an ex-Southampton Guy Arab that had red and white gingham-patterned Fablon on the seat backs, whilst another had black and white lino tiles on the floor! During the early 'Seventies, in an effort to update the fleet, a number of Leyland Leopard single-deckers were purchased from Southdown, and some Park Royal-bodied AEC Regent Vs from City of Oxford.

Also at Fareham were to be seen the standard Bristol/ECW buses of Hants & Dorset in their standard Tilling-green and cream livery, although even here there were sometimes surprises, such as a prewar Bristol K with heavily rebuilt body.

From Fareham the 45 continued on to Warsash, the westernmost point of the Southdown empire, by which time it was 20 miles or so from the Sussex border.

Left: Southdown had a small depot at Fareham, in which town its vehicles would encounter those of Provincial. Among the latter were a number of prewar AEC Regals rebodied in 1957/8 by local bodybuilder Reading; in this form they gave further service for a number of years, as demonstrated by this view of 25 (CG 9610) at Gosport. Thankfully one has since been preserved. *Kevin Lane / Southdown Enthusiasts' Club*

Left: Provincial's characterful double-deck fleet included 47 (DOR 921), a Park Royal-bodied AEC Regent delivered just before the war, in 1939. This 1950s view shows it at Gosport bus station, with Portsmouth Docks in the background (right). *V. C. Jones / Southdown Enthusiasts' Club*

Right: Until 1929 Provincial had operated trams between Fareham and Gosport. In the postwar era there remained much to interest the enthusiast, as apparent from this view of Reading-bodied Guy Arab 70 (SCG 622) at the company's depot at Hoeford. The traditional scroll fleetname employed by the hitherto independent Provincial company was similar in style to that of BET-owned Southdown, although by 1974, when the photograph was taken, both companies were part of the National Bus Company. *John Bishop*

Right: In NBC ownership Provincial received a number of vehicles second-hand from fellow subsidiaries, and among those transferred was Southdown Leyland Leopard/Marshall 105 (105 CUF), which became Provincial 29 and is seen leaving Gosport bus station in the summer of 1974; note the simplified fleetname. From here one could connect with the ferry to Portsmouth in the background. *John Bishop*

Left: At Fareham Southdown's buses met those not only of independent Provincial but also of state-owned Hants & Dorset, which company had a depot and bus station in the town centre. This mid-1950s view features two classic vehicles, both on Bristol K-type chassis; delivered in 1942 with a wartime Park Royal utility body and converted to open-top postwar, Provincial 54 (ECG 622) makes an interesting comparison with Hants & Dorset 1035 (ERU 586), new in 1939 with Eastern Coach Works bodywork. *D. A. Jones / London Trolleybus Preservation Society*

Left: Having left Fareham, Southdown route 45 penetrated further into Hampshire, to Warsash, deep in Hants & Dorset territory, this being the result of an acquisition in 1930. Seen in the early 1960s, East Lancs-bodied Leyland Titan PD2/12 796 (RUF 196) of 1957 begins the last leg of its journey from Portsmouth, negotiating the railway bridge at Titchfield Road, Fareham; note (on the left) the old-style roadsign, with small red triangle warning of the height restriction, and (right) the advertisement featuring a lady drinking a pint of Courage beer! *R. F. Mack*

3. INTO HAMPSHIRE (2) — THE SCENIC ROUTE

Far right: A busy scene in Brighton in the summer of 1963, and a view which when received back from Kodak was nearly assigned to the waste bin. Today it speaks volumes, with a Leyland PD3, 917 (6917 CD), having completed the long journey from Southsea, pulling up by Pool Valley with full rear blind display for route 31. An open-top BH&D Lodekka on route 17 to Rottingdean prepares to overtake, whilst in the opposite direction Guy Arab 421 (GUF 121) sets off for Devil's Dyke and prepares to overtake the Ford Anglia 105E in the foreground. In the days before the 'Mods & Rockers' riots in Brighton we see an AJS motorcycle and a Lambretta scooter in peaceful harmony! *John Bishop*

As well as the 31, four more Southdown services started from Pool Valley and travelled westwards along Brighton and Hove seafronts. The 9 and 10 followed the 31 route as far as Shoreham, where they crossed the old wooden toll bridge and continued via the A27 to North Lancing, serving Lancing railway station before joining the coast road for the run into Worthing. From there both continued to Patching, where they separated, the 9 turning south, passing through East Preston and Angmering, to its terminus at Littlehampton. The 10 continued along the A27 to Arundel, where one could explore the antique shops, visit the castle, take a boat on the river or go for a trip on one of the country's shortest bus routes, Southdown's 70A, which ran from the bus station to Fitzalan Road and took all of four minutes! At the other end of the scale, during the summer months the return trip to Brighton could be by open-top Guy or PD3 on service 102, reputedly the longest open-top service in the country.

The terrain covered by services 9 and 10 was fairly flat, and for many years they were the preserve of the somewhat under-powered Leyland PD1s, both the all-Leyland variety and those with semi-utility Park Royal bodywork. These gave way to PD2s and eventually the ubiquitous 'Queen Mary' PD3s. Car 257, the first of two PD3s with wrap-around windscreen, was a regular performer on these services, but by then they had been diverted away from Brighton seafront; when the Brighton Area Transport Services (BATS) agreement came into effect in 1961 both were re-routed to run via Brighton station, Seven Dials and the Old Shoreham Road.

For many years there were only five single-deck routes operated in Brighton, these being the 30, 32 and 36 on the Haywards Heath corridor (of which more anon), the 27 to Devil's Dyke and Henfield and the 21. The last worked between Pool Valley and Shoreham Beach, again starting its journey via the coast road as far as Southwick; it then turned north into Kingston Lane, passing under a low railway bridge that precluded the use of double-deckers, and continued to Shoreham by way of Old Shoreham Road, crossing the Norfolk Bridge and terminating on the Shoreham Beach estate. During the late 'Forties the service was worked by glorious Harrington-bodied Leyland Tiger TS7s. These were replaced in the early 'Fifties by the first underfloor-engined single-deckers — Leyland Royal Tigers

with rear- or centre-entrance bodywork by East Lancs; always favourites of the authors, these allowed spotty schoolboys to sit 'up front' beside the driver! Under the BATS agreement the route was replaced partly by the diversion of services 9 and 10 outlined above and partly by the extension of Brighton, Hove & District service 2, which saw Bristol KSWs and Lodekkas venturing onto Shoreham Beach for the first time.

The final Southdown service to use Brighton and Hove seafronts was the 22. This always seemed something of a Cinderella route, for, at its peak, it took a little over three hours from end to end yet it never gained the prestige of the coastal services. Whereas most trunk services were either 'Leyland' or 'Guy', the 22 often had a mixture of both, and it is difficult to specify a particular vehicle type as being typical; TDs, Guys, PD1s, PD2s all operated on the service at one time or another. It also seemed to be one of those routes that was always being lengthened or shortened; over the years it generally turned at Petworth or Midhurst, but at its longest it reached Petersfield, again over the border into Hampshire. Alternate journeys worked 'shorts' between Brighton and Steyning.

The 22 was a particularly pretty route, passing through some of the most attractive West Sussex villages. Having followed the 31 route as far as Shoreham it turned inland, passed the Beeding cement works, where everything in the immediate vicinity was covered in a layer of white dust, and continued through Bramber to the small town of Steyning. Here it would meet up with the two-hourly service 80 to Horsham, a single-deck route on which could be found ECW-bodied Leyland PS1s demoted from express work and, latterly, Leyland Tiger Cubs with attractive Park Royal or Duple (Nudd Bros) bodywork, which vehicles always seemed elusive, especially in the Brighton area.

Southdown was renowned for its connecting services, and at most of the major towns served by the 22 passengers had the chance to change onto other routes. At Washington a connection would be made with service 2 from Worthing to Horsham, while service 1, also from Worthing, would join the 22 as far as Storrington, divert for a while, then rejoin it at Pulborough. At Petworth there would be a connection with the 63 from Chichester to Horsham, and at Midhurst the 60 from

Left: Southdown routes 22 to Petersfield and 31 to Southsea were duplicated as far as Portslade by Brighton, Hove & District's open-top seafront route 17. This view, recorded in the summer of 1955, features the latter's 5994 (EHY 581), a 1938 Bristol K5G/ECW acquired from Bristol Tramways in 1955 and rebuilt to convertible open-top in BH&D's own workshops in Conway Street, Hove. The bus is seen near the Brighton/Hove boundary at Brunswick Terrace, the Regency architecture contrasting markedly with art-deco Embassy Court, the extensive restoration of which was completed in 2005. *John Bishop*

Below: For part of Brighton and Hove seafront the 22 was duplicated by BH&D route 8 from West Street in Brighton to Boundary Road in Hove. In this charming scene, recorded near Hove's King Alfred swimming baths in the early 1960s, an elderly resident assists his female companion from Eastern Coach Works-bodied Bristol K5G 402 (EAP 10) of 1948. Note the advertisement for the joint Southdown/Royal Blue express coach service to Bournemouth and the West Country. The Standard Atlas van just visible on the right recalls a generation of light commercials long vanished from our roads. *Peter J. Relf*

Left: Until the late 1960s route 22 would depart from Pool Valley on the three-hour journey to Petersfield, during which it would pass through some of the most beautiful countryside in Britain. In full lined-out livery, 739 (LUF 239), an all-Leyland Titan PD2/12 of 1952, turns right out of 'the Valley' towards Shoreham, where it would head inland. Royal York Buildings, visible in the background, housed all the vehicle records for the County Borough of Brighton, where Southdown's buses and coaches were registered. *W. J. Haynes / Southdown Enthusiasts' Club*

Above: The High Street in Shoreham-by-Sea, West Sussex, was the point where Southdown routes to Steyning parted company with the coastal route 31 to Worthing and beyond. The presence of modern-looking flats and shops suggests this to be a relatively recent view, but the Brickwoods Ales advertisement on the side of all-Leyland Titan PD2/12 714 (KUF 714) dates it to the early 1960s. New in 1951, the bus was among the last open-platform double-deckers delivered to Southdown; from the following year all new buses arrived with platform doors — a feature which marked a leap forward in terms of passenger comfort and with which 714 and its contemporaries were soon fitted. The informative route/destination display, despite the fact that 714's days were by now numbered, bears testimony to Southdown's high standards. *Malcolm Keeping*

Above: Storrington, in West Sussex, had a small bus station, seen in this view, recorded in the early 1960s, of car 1517 (MCD 517). The vehicle is an East Lancs-bodied Leyland Royal Tiger dating from 1953 (this and the previous batch being known collectively as the '15xx' class) and in 1959 had been rebuilt from centre-to front-entrance layout for one-person operation. Route 71, which linked Arundel with Horsham, was very rural for much of its length and as such was an early candidate for withdrawal, although at this time an hourly frequency was maintained during the day. *Malcolm Keeping*

Left: Between Pulborough and Petworth is the village of Stopham, well known locally for its mediæval bridge, built in 1423 to replace a ferry which hitherto had been the only means of crossing the Arun at this point. The narrowness of the bridge latterly proved something of an impediment to traffic, as demonstrated by this 1969 view of Brighton-bound Leyland PD2/12/ East Lancs 798 (RUF 198) crossing with the aid of traffic lights, but not until the 1980s would a new bridge be built to alleviate the situation. *D. Fereday Glenn*

Above: On its way to/from Petersfield Southdown's route 22 passed through Midhurst, focus for a network of rural routes operated by the independent Hants & Sussex concern and typified by this charming early-postwar scene; if only one knew of the circumstances requiring the passengers to transfer to the vehicle behind. No 49 (DR 9064), a lowbridge Park Royal-bodied Dennis Lance, originated with Plymouth Corporation in 1931, being acquired during the war (in 1944) and withdrawn in 1949. *The Omnibus Society*

Right: A chance photograph taken on 18 April 1969 at Petersfield station, terminus for Southdown's lengthy route 22 from Brighton. By this time the original Hants & Sussex empire had long since crumbled away, and B. S. (Basil) Williams was now operating under the name of Southern Motorways. He was quick to take advantage of the sale of London Transport's 1953-built GS-class ECW-bodied Guy Specials, which proved ideal for services in this sparsely populated area; seen on layover between journeys on service 3 is one-time GS43 (MXX 343). Just visible on the right of the picture is Aldershot & District 555 (MOR 601), a 1954 AEC Reliance rebodied by Metro-Cammell in 1967, which had arrived from Alton on service 53. *John Bishop*

Bognor Regis and Chichester, which also ran to Petersfield but via a different route. For a while services 22 and 60 interworked, buses working through to Bognor and back before returning to Brighton.

Midhurst was also the starting-point for several Hants & Sussex routes, particularly those to Graffham, Lurgashall and Treyford, these routes surviving into the late 'Seventies, by which time they were being worked by dual-door Marshall-bodied AEC Swifts acquired from Portsmouth Corporation. Lowbridge double-deckers had been used in earlier years, ranging from former Plymouth Corporation Dennis Lances with Weymann or Park Royal bodies to Leyland PD1s with lowbridge Northern Coachbuilders bodies, bought new in 1947. The list

of vehicles operated by Hants & Sussex reads like a preservationist's dream, and it is impossible to mention all the types that could be seen in postwar years.

At Midhurst one could also catch a glimpse of an Aldershot & District AEC Reliance on service 19, in shades of green and cream similar to Southdown's but differently applied. But it was at Petersfield, terminus of the 22, that A&D buses really became apparent, operating from the town on the 6 to Aldershot, the 24 to Guildford and the 53 to Alton.

Aldershot & District was very faithful to Dennis Bros of Guildford for its double-deckers and, indeed, for its single-deckers too until the

Above: Activity in this superb view at Guildford's Farnham Road bus station in the spring of 1969. On the right 355 (SOU 463), an East Lancs-bodied Dennis Loline, waits to depart on route 24 to Petersfield, where it would meet Southdown vehicles from the south; the two single-deckers are Weymann-bodied AEC Reliances, both still with original scroll fleetnames, which look so much better than the simplified version on 355. *Dave Brown*

Left: Another prominent independent and one-time part of the Hants & Sussex empire was Liss & District, which operated a stage-carriage service from Liss to Liphook. One of the interesting vehicles acquired by the new owners after the business was sold was this AEC Regent III, the chassis of which dated from 1946 and had been retained by AEC for experimental purposes; in 1959 it was given a forward-entrance lowbridge body by Roe and registered as VHO 123, in which form it is seen on Brighton's Madeira Drive during that year's British Coach Rally. *Glyn Kraemer-Johnson collection*

Left: Delivered in 1958, Southdown's first Northern Counties-bodied Leyland Titan PD3s represented an immense step forward in design whilst maintaining all the company's traditional quality. No 817 (TCD 817) was one of the first batch of 15, delivered before the nickname 'Queen Mary' was adopted, and would spend the majority of its career in the Portsmouth area; nearly four years old by the time this view was recorded on 5 October 1962, it is seen at The Square, Petersfield, on route 42, which ran to/from Portsmouth via the A3 main London Road. *Alan Lambert / Southdown Enthusiasts' Club*

advent of the underfloor-engined chassis, with which, for some reason, Dennis had little success. Mainstay of the double-deck fleet for many years was the Dennis Loline, a Bristol Lodekka built under licence, and the original Lolines with rear-entrance East Lancs bodywork must have been amongst the most handsome buses of this layout to be built. The later forward-entrance Weymann body, as built on A&D's Loline IIIs, was probably the most attractive variant of the MCW Orion family, only the Alexander version letting the side down with its bulbous roof.

Petersfield was also the northernmost point of the Portsmouth Joint Transport Area, being served by services 40 and 42 to/from Southsea. There was also an independent, Liss & District, which operated a service from Petersfield to Longmoor. Liss & District had been part of the Hants & Sussex empire, but was sold off in 1954. By the late 'Fifties it was under the control of Creamline of Bordon, vehicles sporting an attractive livery of pale blue and grey. Two of its most

interesting vehicles used on this service were AEC Regent IIIs with experimental chassis (built *c*1946) on which were built forward-entrance lowbridge bodies by Roe. The first (VHO 123), completed early in 1959, was of traditional half-cab design, with elegant AEC radiator; the second (150 AOU) appeared at the end of the following year and, whilst virtually identical in all other respects, had a full-width cab and Regent V radiator grille that jarred with the good looks of the traditional Roe body. Unusual by any standards, such buses were quite a shock to encounter unexpectedly in a country town on the Sussex/Hampshire border.

Another incongruous sight to be seen for a while in Petersfield was a former Hastings single-deck trolleybus, which Southdown had acquired and converted into a mobile enquiry office. Towed around to wherever it was required, it spent a couple of years in Petersfield while a new travel office was being constructed.

4. CARFAX — THE MEETING PLACE

Right: In 1955 Southdown turned to Guy Motors for an initial batch of 12 Guy Arab IVs with handsome Park Royal bodywork. Having arrived in Brighton on route 17 from Horsham, 520 (OUF 520) is seen near journey's end, approaching Edward Street, the location for Southdown's main depot in the town. Complete with dark-green lining, the bus is in 'as delivered' condition, even down to the letter 'H' below the fleet number (just discernible behind the rear wheel arch), denoting that the bus has a highbridge body; both suffix and lining would be lost on repaint. *Eric Surfleet / Southdown Enthusiasts' Club*

Far right: Designs come and go, but few rears can match the lines of the prewar Weymann design, as seen in this night-time view of 1939 Brighton Corporation AEC trolleybus 4 (FUF 4) standing at the Old Steine between journeys on Hollingbury route 46 in May 1961; just visible in front, deputising for a trolleybus on route 46A, is 71 (WCD 71), a Leyland PD2 with later design of Weymann body. Note how the Corporation used every available space to maximise revenue from advertising! *John Bishop*

Horsham was the nearest 'border' town to Brighton and could be reached in two ways. By rail, the 'Horsham Flyer' was one of the comparatively few steam-hauled services from Brighton, usually consisting of three coaches hauled by a BR Standard or 'M7'-class tank engine. Horsham trains left the coast line at Shoreham and ran via Steyning, Partridge Green and West Grinstead, more or less paralleling Southdown's service 80 (Steyning–Horsham). It was logical, therefore, that when the line was closed to passenger traffic in 1966 the 80 should be extended to Brighton by way of a replacement; as such it became a limited-stop service (renumbered 80X) and was operated largely by Marshall-bodied Leyland Tiger Cubs.

The other service between Brighton and Horsham was the 17. In the early postwar years this was operated by a mixture of rebodied Leyland

TDs, but in 1955/6 Southdown took delivery of 48 splendid Park Royal-bodied Guy Arab IVs, which were allocated to most of the major inland routes throughout the system. Service 17 was one such and was maintained by the Guys for many years until, like most of the more rural services, it was converted to one-man single-deck operation.

The 17 left Pool Valley, mingling with Brighton Corporation trolleybuses as it made its way along London Road to Preston Circus. There the trolleybuses on services 46/46A branched off to the right, effortlessly climbing Beaconsfield Villas to Preston Drove and Hollingbury. Brighton's trams had been abandoned in 1939 and replaced by 44 trolleybuses and 21 motor buses, all of AEC manufacture, and all with bodywork by Weymann of basically similar design. In the late 'Forties these prewar vehicles were joined by 14 AEC Regent IIIs and eight BUT trolleybuses, again all with Weymann bodywork. Withdrawal of the trolleybuses began in 1959 and was completed in June 1961, Weymann-bodied Leyland PD2s taking over.

From Preston Circus the 17 ran in company with the Brighton, Hove & District Bristol Ks and Lodekkas on the 5 and 15 group of services to Patcham. Although under the BATS agreement the boundary of the Brighton area was set at Pyecombe, Patcham remained the most northerly point reached by BH&D. (The agreement did, however, have an effect on Southdown's service 17. Operating within the Brighton area were two pairs of routes with the same route number, these being the 14 and 17, so to avoid confusion BH&D's 14 was renumbered 54 while Southdown's 17 became the 117. BH&D's 17 was, of course, the famous seafront open-top service.)

Left: Mere weeks before withdrawal, Brighton Corporation AEC/Weymann trolleybus 23 (FUF 23) stands at the Old Steine, on Whit Monday (22 May) 1961, waiting to depart on route 46A. Alongside is another Weymann body but mounted on an AEC Regent motor-bus chassis. The paintwork on the trolleybus looks somewhat jaded by now, only essential maintenance being carried out by the staff at Lewes Road depot ahead of complete closure of the system at the end of June 1961. *John Bishop*

Above: After the initial batch of 44 AEC trolleybuses for Brighton Corporation in 1939 postwar extensions dictated a demand for another batch of trolleybuses, resulting in the delivery in 1947 of a further six vehicles, distinguishable by their flush-fitting destination screens (as opposed to the protruding displays on prewar vehicles). Seen in Grand Parade, shared with Southdown vehicles, 50 (HUF 50) nears the end of its journey on circular route 42 via Queen's Park, passing a fine display of contemporary British motorcycles as it approaches the Old Steine. No 50 would be sold to Bradford Corporation in 1959, after the first stage of trolleybus abandonment. *Photobus*

Right: An oft-neglected aspect of bus photography (given how bus design has changed in the past 50 years) is the rear view, as here in Brighton's Old Steine. Nearest the camera is one-time Brighton, Hove & District 499 (MPM 499), one of the last K types built (in 1957) and of added interest in being a KS6G model built to 7ft 6in width (rather than the usual 8ft) to enable it to negotiate St James's Street. By the time this scene was recorded in June 1971 BH&D had been taken over by Southdown and this bus, by now renumbered 2499, was very near the end of its life. *Dave Brown*

Far right: Brighton's Old Steine would always present the perfect opportunity to photograph buses on layover between duties. Delivered in 1969, this 33ft Daimler Fleetline was ordered for the main Southdown fleet but diverted to the BH&D fleet as 2111 (PUF 211H). Despite representing a radical departure from the hitherto standard ECW, the handsome lines of its Northern Counties bodywork and full destination display combined with the superb BH&D livery to ensure it looked 'right'. *John Bishop*

From Patcham the 17's journey was fairly solitary. It turned off the A23 at Pyecombe and at Henfield met up with the 27, which had travelled from Brighton via Devil's Dyke and Poynings. At Cowfold a connection was made with service 81 to Haywards Heath, and at Pronger's Corner it was joined by the 89, also from Haywards Heath, for the final run into Horsham.

Horsham is an attractive town, and the Carfax, at its centre, was (until the opening of the new bus station in 2003) the meeting place for a number of bus operators. Prominent amongst the 'big boys' was London Transport, whose green Country Area RTs (and before that STLs) ran into the town on service 405 from Croydon and the 414 from Dorking. RFs operated the 434 to Crawley and East Grinstead and the

473 to Dormansland, having taken over in 1953 from those beautiful all-time classics, the 10T10s. Here too were more single-deck Reliances of Aldershot & District, on its service 33 to Guildford. But it was the independents that generated the greatest interest.

Over the years the independent operators came and went, and routes were extended, shortened, replaced and passed from one operator to another. In the space at our disposal we can taste but a *soupçon* of the fascinating vehicles that were to be seen in the period covered by this book.

Hants & Sussex was once again very much in evidence with its services to Plaistow, Roffey and Three Bridges, the routes being licensed to F. H. Kilner, a business taken over by Hants & Sussex

Left: By October 1975, when this view was recorded, Aldershot & District had been amalgamated with one-time Tilling subsidiary Thames Valley, to form Thames Valley & Aldershot, better known as Alder Valley. Seen on layover near Horsham station, Bristol RE 437 (YHO 621J) still retained A&D livery (minus fleetname, hence the blank cream panel above the front wheel-arch), making for an interesting comparison with traditional Southdown livery; shortly afterwards it would succumb to the poppy red seen on the vehicle just visible in front. *John Bishop*

in 1945. Leyland PD1 FCG 525, with highbridge body by Northern Coachbuilders, was a regular performer on the Roffey service, while Bedford OBs with Duple bus bodies tended to operate the other two. This all came to an end in December 1954, when the Kilner business ceased trading. The Plaistow route was replaced by Aldershot & District's 50A, whilst the Roffey service was covered by a variant of London Transport's 434. London Transport also came to the rescue with the introduction of its 852 service between Ewhurst, Horsham, Three Bridges and Crawley, but, following objections that it was operating outside its prescribed area, the Ewhurst–Horsham section was handed over to Brown Motor Services, leaving the Horsham–Crawley section to London Transport, which operated it with a single GS-class Guy Special 26-seater.

An old-established Horsham independent was Mitchell of Warnham, which in the postwar years operated two main services, from Horsham to Rusper via Holbrook and from Horsham to Ockley via Broadbridge Heath and Warnham. Mitchell's vehicles wore a livery of green and cream until 1964, when it was changed to dark red and grey, although from the 1950s some vehicles were given a basically cream livery. Again, an interesting fleet was operated. During the war the company had acquired a Dennis Pike from Yellow Bus Services of Guildford, together with two new Bedford

OWBs. In the late 'Forties two Maudslay Marathon III coaches joined the fleet, one with Whitson coachwork, the other Plaxton. In 1950 came a Leyland PS1 with rare King & Taylor coach body, but probably the most interesting acquisition was a Leyland Comet with Duple coach body. As in so many cases, dwindling traffic brought about the company's demise and in June 1973 it was sold to Compact Coaches of Crawley.

Another long-established operator much in evidence during the 'Fifties and 'Sixties was A. T. Brady, trading as Brown Motor Services, known locally as 'the Brown Baby' or 'the Brownie'. Again, the services changed over the years, but latterly the main operation was a route from Forest Green to Horsham via Ewhurst, Wallis Wood and Broadbridge Heath. The Brown Motor Services fleet was, hardly surprisingly, painted brown and cream, and also included some interesting vehicles. Before World War 2 Bedford WTBs had been favoured. In 1943/4 two Bedford OWBs with Duple bus bodies had been purchased, and in postwar years that favourite of all independents, the Bedford OB, had been chosen. However, here too was a Leyland Comet, again with Duple body, purchased new in 1950 and registered OPB 536. In 1959 Brady purchased another unusual bus for a small operator, this being an Albion Nimbus with Willowbrook

bus body, which in spite of the model's sometimes dubious reputation served him well for 11 years.

The last Brown Motor Services bus ran on 31 October 1970, following which the business passed to North Downs Rural Transport. In 1969 North Downs had taken over Mitchell's route from Horsham to Ockley using a Bedford C5Z1 with 29-seat Duple Vista body. Together with Brady's route 852 North Downs acquired both the Leyland Comet and the Albion Nimbus, the latter subsequently being joined by three further examples bought from Western Welsh. North Downs also operated a large number of Bristols, including LS5G buses and LS6G coaches.

There would be many more route alterations before the Horsham services were passed on once again, this time to Tillingbourne Valley. Tillingbourne continued the practice of operating an interesting fleet, working the Horsham–Broadbridge Heath–Warnham service with an ex-London Transport GS and a Bristol SU from Western National. Tillingbourne continued to operate Horsham local services until the company went into administration in 2001.

Before leaving Horsham, a trip to the Southdown garage would usually be well rewarded; it was here that the company stored many of its withdrawn vehicles that were awaiting disposal, and one could usually catch a final glimpse of a once-famous type before it disappeared forever.

Left: Southdown also operated local services from Horsham, as demonstrated by 155 (EUF 155), a 1938 Leyland TD5 rebodied postwar by Beadle, at the Carfax. Route 78 operated between Balcombe (near Haywards Heath) and Horsham and would be an early candidate for pruning. The Southdown office shared with Aldershot & District is seen in the background on the left. Note once again the Southdown practice of affixing the registration plate between decks, even though provision is made below the radiator.
John Bishop collection

Left: A final view at Horsham Carfax, featuring 1529 (MCD 529), an East Lancs-bodied Leyland Royal Tiger of 1953, basking in the sun in May 1961. The body has been converted from centre- to front-entrance to permit one-person operation, and regrettably its dark-green roof has been overpainted; nevertheless, the beading has been retained, as has the 'Southdown' badge on the front.
Alan Lambert / Southdown Enthusiasts' Club

47

Above: A prewar view of lowbridge Beadle-bodied Leyland TD5 189 (EUF 189) of 1938 in Brighton's Pool Valley bus station, showing the standard expected of Southdown. Given today's low-floor buses one forgets the sunken side gangway on the upper deck, necessary to achieve the lowbridge designs of yesteryear. Note (on the right) the open-top Brush-bodied Leyland TD1, 809 (UF 4809), which dated from 1929 but would see continued service postwar. *Eric Surfleet / Southdown Enthusiasts' Club*

It was but a short ride — not much more than half an hour or so — by London Transport RT from Horsham to Crawley, which made it quite simple to complete a round-trip, returning to Brighton by Southdown service 23.

The 23 was another of those routes that had been worked by a variety of rebodied prewar Leyland TDs; in fact this writer's first journey on the route was on a lowbridge example. However, when the Guy Arab IVs arrived, the 23 was one of the first routes to receive them.

The 23 left Brighton by the same route as the 17, but at Pyecombe, instead of turning left, it veered to the right, passing the Jack and Jill windmills and, as it crossed the main London–Brighton railway line, allowing a glimpse of the entrance to the famous Clayton Tunnel, with its turreted and castellated portal. It followed the railway line as far as Hassocks and then served Ditchling and Wivelsfield before running into Haywards Heath.

Haywards Heath was once very much a Southdown stronghold. In the company's heyday in the 'Fifties and 'Sixties it served as a crossing-point for east–west and north–south services. In the 'Fifties a fine bus station was built in contemporary style close to the railway station, and many bus photographs taken at this location have the familiar water tower in the background. Buses to be seen here were a fair representation of the Southdown fleet — Park Royal Guys on 'main line' services 23 and 89, with TDs and (later) PD2s on the more local services. Then there were the three single-deck routes from Brighton, the 30, 32 and 36, maintained for many years by East Lancs-bodied Leyland Royal Tigers. The 123 from Haywards Heath to Lewes and Newhaven always seemed to be associated with Leyland PD1s, especially the Park Royal-bodied variety. Haywards Heath bus station was also noteworthy in that one of the Beadle-bodied Leyland Tiger Cubs was stationed there for many years as a 'left luggage' office until, unfortunately, it was destroyed by fire.

While the 23 continued on from Haywards Heath to Crawley via Handcross and Pease Pottage, a two-hourly service numbered 82 ran between the same points but via Balcombe and Worth.

Crawley was very much London Transport territory. In the early 'Fifties it bore little resemblance to the flourishing New Town of today; not only was the town itself very much smaller, but the massive

complex that was to be Gatwick Airport had yet to be built. Superb though its vehicles were, the London Transport fleet of the time was boring, to say the least, with thousands of RT-family double-deckers, hundreds of RF single-deckers and not much else. The Country Area could boast its 75 GS-class normal-control Guys, with 26-seat bodywork by Eastern Coach Works, but these were spread pretty thinly.

Crawley was little different vehicle-wise from anywhere else in the Country Area. By the early 'Fifties STLs, Qs and Ts had largely been replaced by RTs and RFs, together with a handful of GSs brought in for services 473 and 852. There were also some RFs in a different livery, these being the Green Line coaches that worked the 710 from Crawley to Baker Street. This had started in prewar days as route I, operating from Crawley to Watford, but was cut back to Baker Street when Green Line services were resumed after the war; in 1947 it was extended northwards to Amersham. In 1968 the portion between Crawley and Baker Street was withdrawn following the introduction the previous year of service 727; an orbital service starting from

Crawley then connecting Gatwick, Heathrow and Luton airports, this was worked for a while in the late 'Sixties by the RC-class AEC Reliances with Willowbrook bodies to standard BET design.

The building of the New Town begun in the early 'Fifties had brought about changes to existing services and the introduction of new routes to serve the new housing and industrial estates, an example of the latter being the 483, introduced in 1953 between Crawley (The George) and Northgate. By 1958 the New Town was beginning to develop south of the railway line in what was traditionally Southdown territory, and a mileage-based agreement was therefore drawn up, enabling each operator to serve both parts of the town and thus provide cross-town services. As a result London Transport route 483 was withdrawn, being replaced by an extension of Southdown's 23 to Northgate and the introduction of a new service 23A between Pease Pottage, Crawley and Northgate.

For a while during 1961/2 there was an added incentive to visit the LT garage in that T787, the very last T-class AEC Regal to remain in

Above: How are the mighty fallen! Seen near the entrance to
Haywards Heath bus station in the 1960s, 704 (KUF 704), an all-
Leyland PD2/12 dating from 1951, would originally have been used
on 'main road' routes, but the advent of newer vehicles demoted this
once proud vehicle to the rural 82 from Haywards Heath to Crawley,
which ran to a two-hourly frequency. The scene has changed
very little 40 years on, being instantly recognisable today.
Malcolm Keeping

Left: Opened in 1956, Haywards Heath bus station was a centre for Southdown's Mid Sussex routes. Marshall-bodied Bristol RELL 446 (NUF 446G) is seen *c*1973 on route 89, which ran on an hourly headway between Horsham and Uckfield, the full journey taking nearly three hours. Today it has been reduced to just a handful of journeys between Horsham and Haywards Heath and is thus but a shadow of its former self. *Malcolm Keeping*

Left: Journey's end for route 23 in Crawley High Street, where buses parked in the centre of the road. Here the immaculate all-Leyland PD2, 736 (LUF 236) of 1952, would meet with London Transport Country Area buses. Note the temporary London Transport stop behind the passengers. The shelter on the left is a common LT-style shelter that could be seen throughout the London area. *Eric Surfleet / Southdown Enthusiasts' Club*

Right: Crawley was one of a number of 'border' towns where Southdown territory adjoined London Transport's Country Area. RT2516 (KXW 145) is seen basking in the sunshine in the High Street in the days before the Routemaster family ruled the roads in and around London. Note the coin-operated weighing machine outside Dixey's opticians. *Eric Surfleet*

Below: Another classic London Transport type to be seen in Crawley was the 10T10 AEC Regal with Chiswick-built body. However, by the early 1950s, when this photograph was taken, T463 (ELP 187) had been demoted from Green Line duties to bus work, the brackets above the side windows being now devoid of the route boards once carried. *R. H. G. Simpson*

Right: In May 1962, armed with camera, a young John Bishop made a chance trip to Crawley, where, allowed within the confines of the London Transport garage, he discovered an added bonus in the form of ECW-bodied Guy Special GS12 (MXX 312). Standing next to it in the back yard, in a slightly lighter shade of green, was Green Line AEC Regal IV/Metro-Cammell RF51 (LYF 402). Both vehicles would regularly have encountered Southdown buses. *John Bishop*

53

Right: In the early 1960s a purpose-built bus station was opened at Crawley which, although not quite as central as the High Street, removed the hazard to passengers of passing traffic. This deceptively rural view, with substantial trees surrounding the area, features Southdown 175 (KCD 175F), one of a large number of Leyland Leopard saloons with bodywork to BET Federation design (built in this case by Marshall of Cambridge) delivered in the years 1963-8 and which would give yeoman service to the company. Following extensive rebuilding of Crawley town centre in the 1980s this area is now occupied by the large County Mall shopping centre, a new bus station having been built in a slightly more central location nearby. *J. Chisholm / Southdown Enthusiasts' Club*

Right: Until Gatwick Airport was expanded to include a coach station Southdown had its own at County Oak, Crawley, where passengers travelling between London and the South Coast could pause before continuing their journey. This view features Worthing-bound Leyland Tiger Cub/ Beadle 1067 (RUF 67) of 1956 keeping company with a pair of half-cab Leyland Tiger PS1s. Note the provision for roof boards to display destinations, albeit not fitted in this view. Towards the end of its existence the rear of the coach station would play host to redundant vehicles, affording enthusiasts the opportunity to pay their last respects, but the entire site has long since disappeared beneath urban redevelopment in this commercially prosperous area. *Southdown Enthusiasts' Club (photographer not recorded)*

Right: Crawley High Street was the terminus for Southdown routes 82 from Haywards Heath and 23 from Brighton; there was also a small nucleus of routes operated in the town and out to Pease Pottage to the south, until these were 'rationalised' in the 1970s. Southdown still had a presence at the office in Crawley bus station when this view was recorded on 6 February 1975, but prominent in this view is one of London Country's unloved 'Merlins' (AEC Swifts), MBS436 (VLW 436G), dating from 1969 and still in its original London Transport green (albeit with waistband repainted yellow in lieu of the original cream), standing between an unidentified rebuilt Green Line RF and Routemaster RCL2253, recently repainted in NBC leaf green. *John Bishop*

service with London Transport, was allocated to Crawley and could often be seen in the yard.

As far as Southdown was concerned Crawley was noteworthy for its Coach Station at County Oak. Built in 1931, it wasn't a coach station in the accepted sense but served as a halfway refreshment and comfort stop for coaches on express services between London and Brighton or Worthing; it was also sometimes used by excursion coaches. And what a wonderful sight it presented over the years! In the late 'Forties and early 'Fifties one would be greeted by a line of gleaming half-cabs, including prewar Leyland Tiger TS8s and postwar PS1s. The latter had bodywork by a variety of coachbuilders, including Duple, Harrington, Beadle, Park Royal and Windover, but most commonly used on the London–Brighton service were those bodied by Eastern Coach Works, which firm's 'express' body, with stepped waistband, looked particularly well in Southdown livery. Delivered with ECW's standard

sliding ventilators, they soon had these replaced by a rather unusual type of half-drop window and thus became unique to Southdown.

In the mid-'Fifties express services were largely taken over by Beadle-Commer integrals. Attractive coaches, they were quite different in outline from the 130 Tiger Cubs bodied by the same coachbuilder. They were fitted with Commer's TS3 two-stroke three-cylinder engine, which was extremely economical, and their throaty engine note and rasping exhaust made them instantly recognisable long before the vehicle came into sight. There followed Leyland Tiger Cubs with attractive Weymann Fanfare coachwork and then the all-conquering Leyland Leopard.

Eventually, with the building of the airport, Gatwick became the important stopping-point for coaches; not long afterwards Southdown's glorious apple green was replaced by the unimaginative National white, and another era came to an end.

6. THE THIRTY-SOMETHINGS

Far right: Pool Valley, Brighton, always appeared the centre of the Southdown 'empire', with routes radiating in all directions and from where passengers would start their journey to the rural extremities of Sussex. By the time this view of 'Queen Mary' Leyland PD3/Northern Counties 250 (BUF 250C) was recorded in the early 1970s evidence of state ownership had crept in by the advertisements on the front of the vehicle. There was, however, little else to indicate that NBC was now in control as 250 prepared to head east on route 12A to Peacehaven. The Bristol RESL behind, 248 (KUF 248F), was ready for the long journey north to East Grinstead, close to the Surrey border. *Malcolm Keeping*

Right: It seemed as though at least one vehicle belonging to Campings Coaches would always be seen on the seafront at Brighton and this view, just outside Pool Valley bus station, is no exception, featuring PCD 600, an AEC Regal IV with Plaxton coachwork. Behind can be seen a Southdown Leyland Tiger PS1 with Park Royal body rebuilt with full front. The board leaning against the wheel (to avoid damaging the paintwork) advertises a trip to Winchelsea and Rye for 10s 6d (52½p). *Glyn Kraemer-Johnson collection*

Southdown seemed to have a penchant for cramped bus and coach stations. Situated beneath the company's Head Office, Brighton's coach station was built on an angle between Steine Street and Manchester Street, with barely room for more than half a dozen coaches. Access was via the narrow Manchester Street, which often became blocked by coaches queuing to enter the coach station, and it was not unknown for the tailback to reach busy St James's Street.

Pool Valley was little better. It was approached by a narrow road between two buildings, little wider than the buses themselves. The 'Valley' itself was triangular in shape, the apex being the exit onto the seafront. The base contained the bus stands onto which buses reversed, the conductors hanging off the platforms with one hand on the bell ready to ring it before the back wheels reached the kerb. The west side, beneath the wall of the Savoy cinema, was used to park vehicles out of service, while the central area was quite often occupied by buses waiting for the stands to become vacant. The stand beside the entrance

was used by services to Lewes and beyond, including those operated jointly with Maidstone & District, whilst that at the other end was reserved for the single-deckers on the 30, 32 and 36.

Cramped it may have been, but Pool Valley was certainly central. The 30 group left Brighton by the same route as the 17 and 23 and as they turned left out of Pool Valley they passed, on the right, the Palace Pier, opposite which was the Aquarium. Between the two ran Madeira Drive (finishing-point for the British Coach Rally, the Veteran Car Club run and the Historic Commercial Vehicle rally), along which would be parked a long line of excursion coaches, each with a beautifully chalked board leaning against it to advertise its tour. Southdown's contribution in the early days would have been half-cab Leyland PS1s, these being followed by Royal Tigers, Beadle rebuilds and Beadle-bodied Tiger Cubs. In later years, when Southdown took lightweight vehicles, Harrington- and Burlingham-bodied Commer Avengers would jostle with Weymann Fanfare-bodied Tiger Cubs and Leopards bodied by Harrington to the classic Cavalier style.

As well as Southdown there would be representatives of the three Brighton coach operators — Alpha, Campings and Unique. Alpha and Unique both operated mainly Bedfords, the former's in an all-cream livery, those of Unique in a smart two-tone green. Campings, in the early days (when it was purely a coach operator and not a dealer), had an attractive livery of turquoise and cream and operated several heavyweight AECs — Regal IVs and Reliances — with Plaxton and Burlingham bodies.

Beyond the excursion coaches were the setting-down and pick-up points for the visiting coaches, and on summer Saturdays and Sundays there would be a constant stream of coaches arriving and departing. The classic names of the past were always to be seen — Grey-Green, Orange Luxury, Empire's Best, Fallowfield and Britten — as well as lesser-

Right: Seen when almost new in 1952, an immaculate '15xx' Leyland Royal Tiger/East Lancs, 1505 (LUF 505), stands in Brighton's Pool Valley bus station, in the bay reserved for the '30 group' routes. Fitted with rear doors, this vehicle would later be rebuilt to front-entrance layout. *The Omnibus Society*

Right: The 1953 batch of East Lancs-bodied Royal Tigers featured a centre-entrance layout. Seen in precisely the same spot as car 1505 *(shown above)*, 1518 (MCD 518), was still in original form with dark green roof when photographed in the late 1950s. A ride next to the driver through the rural roads of Sussex would have been a 'must' for any budding enthusiast, but the opportunity would be lost for good when these buses were rebuilt to front-entrance configuration. *John Bishop*

Left: Along the seafront at Brighton, beyond the excursion stops used by local companies, one could find all manner of visiting coaches picking up passengers after a day at the seaside. Seen in the late 1950s, Aldershot & District 197 (LAA 232), a Strachans-bodied Dennis Lancet dating from 1953, awaits the return of its passengers. The full-fronted coachwork was an attempt to make the vehicle look more modern, but close scrutiny reveals the engine to be at the front rather than under the floor. Nevertheless, standing by the (rear) entrance, the driver looks proud of his gleaming charge — and rightly so. *John Bishop*

known independents and a smattering of London Transport RTs and RFs, which always looked a little incongruous with the sea as a backdrop.

The 30 and 32 followed the same route as far as Haywards Heath, travelling via Hassocks and Burgess Hill, whilst the 36 served Keymer instead of Burgess Hill. From Haywards Heath the three services continued via Lindfield and Horsted Keynes to Danehill, where they finally separated. The 30 made the short journey to Chelwood Common, where it terminated, the 32 continuing through Fletching and Piltdown to its terminus at Uckfield.

Uckfield had itself been a 'border town' at one time. Here Southdown had met with the buses of Autocar of Tunbridge Wells and the East Surrey Traction Co, both part of the Underground group. In 1932 the two companies joined to form London General Country Services, and a year later this was absorbed into the London Passenger Transport Board. However, the southern boundary of the London Transport area was set at East Grinstead, Crawley and Horsham, and as a result

Southdown gained the territory west of a line drawn from East Grinstead to Uckfield, that to the east passing to Maidstone & District.

Like Haywards Heath, Uckfield was another of those 'crossroads' where north–south and east–west services met and where Southdown was able to show off its prowess at providing connecting services. Here the 32 would meet up with the 119 and 122 from Brighton to Tunbridge Wells and Gravesend, operated jointly by Southdown and Maidstone & District, the 89 from Horsham, which had also worked through from Haywards Heath but by a different route, the 92 from Hailsham and Eastbourne and the 192, also from Eastbourne but which reached Uckfield via Heathfield and was also joint with M&D. Then there was the 120 to Crowborough and finally Maidstone & District's own 79 to Tunbridge Wells via Buxted and Mayfield, which terminated in the town.

From Horsted Keynes, the third service, the 36, followed the now-famous Bluebell Line through Kingscote and on to journey's end at East Grinstead.

Left: Uckfield bus station on a winter's day in the late 1960s,
in a scene which speaks volumes about the climatic conditions.
Park Royal-bodied Guy Arab IV 516 (OUF 516), with blind set for
route 89 to Horsham, has most of its radiator blanked off in an
attempt to protect the engine from the cold; alongside, East Lancs-
bodied Leyland PD2/12 810 (RUF 210) has newspaper stuffed
between the body and radiator, to keep out the draught.
At this time Uckfield was still a haven for PD2s; note the
Park Royal 'OCD' in the background. *Malcolm Keeping*

Above: The spirit of Southdown's prewar Leyland Tigers
lived on with the Beadle chassisless rebuilds, which proved ideal
for lightly trafficked rural routes. Looking a little the worse
for wear, 648 (MUF 487) of 1953 is seen at Uckfield on a snowy
day, ready for duty on the circuitous route 120 to Crowborough,
via the main A26 road to Tunbridge Wells, Kent. Thankfully 649
(MUF 488) of the same batch has been preserved and can be seen
regularly at bus rallies. *Malcolm Keeping*

East Grinstead was again very much a London Transport stronghold, with the usual mix of RTs, RFs and GSs, together with Green Line RFs that had taken over from 10T10s on the 708, a long cross-London route from East Grinstead to Hemel Hempstead. The most important routes were probably the 409 (Forest Row–East Grinstead–West Croydon) and the 424 (East Grinstead–Reigate). The 424 gained fame in 1965 when it became the first London Transport route to be worked by rear-engined double-deckers.

For its first venture into rear-engined double-deckers London Transport bought 50 Leyland Atlanteans and eight Daimler Fleetlines, all with standard Park Royal bodywork. The Atlanteans were painted red for Central London use, but the Daimlers received Country Area green livery and were allocated to East Grinstead for service 424, although they also worked on the 435 and 438C. At around the same time 100 RMLs were delivered in green for Country Area use, and some were allocated to the 409. The 424 again made headlines when the XFs were temporarily swapped with red XAs for comparative trials and yet again when experiments were carried out with the Fleetlines working as one-man buses during off-peak times. For this a 'gate' had been fitted at the foot of the stairs, and this was closed when there was no conductor on board, the buses effectively running as single-deckers. It was not a practice that was continued.

Maidstone & District also operated on three services from East Grinstead — the 91 to Tunbridge Wells, the 135 to Edenbridge and the

137 to Crowborough. The 91 was usually worked with lowbridge double-deckers, particularly the AEC Regent Vs, while the other two were single-deck routes.

Until 1951 East Grinstead had been home to a long-established independent, H. J. Sargent. Sargent's coaching activities had been absorbed by Southdown as long ago as 1933, and his East Grinstead – Ashdown Forest service was taken over in 1937, becoming the Southdown 87. Sargent's remaining services continued to be operated by faithful Bedford OBs until taken over by Southdown in March 1951; they included works services to Gatwick Airport and Crawley, which were passed to London Transport, which operated them from Crawley garage, initially with 4Q4s.

The 30, 32 and 36 were always operated by single-deckers, on account of a low bridge near Horsted Keynes, although double-deckers occasionally worked reliefs as far as Haywards Heath. Before the advent of the underfloor-engined single-decker they had been worked by the 1400-class Leyland Tiger TS7s with handsome Harrington coachwork, although during the war the six-wheel Leyland TS7Ts normally used on the Beachy Head service were allocated to the 30; in true Southdown tradition they were fitted with fully painted roofboards for the service. In 1952/3 Leyland Royal Tigers with rear- or centre-entrance East Lancs bodies (all later converted to front entrance) took over on all three routes, upon which they remained for many years. In 1960/1 a number of the all-Leyland Royal Tiger coaches were converted to dual-purpose status for bus work, although the only visible alteration was the fitting of a large destination box on the front dome. No route number box was fitted, and with their centre entrances and hand-operated sliding doors they must have been most unsuitable for bus work. Nevertheless, they lasted in this form for about five years before withdrawal and were regular performers on the 30, 32 and 36. In the early 'Sixties Marshall-bodied Leyland Tiger Cubs took over for a while before the ubiquitous 36ft BET Leopard appeared on the scene, and thereafter the three services somehow became anonymous amongst a whole host of services all operated by the same type of vehicle.

Left: Prior to the advent of the '15xx' Leyland Royal Tigers the prewar '14xx' Harrington-bodied Tigers were the staple fare on rural routes in Sussex, including the 30 group (30, 32 and 36). By the mid-1950s, when this view was recorded in Haywards Heath bus station, 1461 (FCD 261) had been demoted to relief duties but still made an impressive sight. It is a matter of great regret that of the 85 delivered not one of these vehicles survived to be preserved. *Eric Surfleet / Southdown Enthusiasts' Club*

Left: In 1934/5 four three-axle Leyland Tigers, with bodywork by Short Bros, were purchased to provide extra capacity on the Eastbourne–Beachy Head route, upon which double-deckers were not then permitted. Following the outbreak of war these machines were no longer required on their regular haunt, and TS7T 553 (BUF 553) was redeployed on routes 30/32/36 between Brighton and Haywards Heath. This classic wartime view shows it at Haywards Heath railway station, with servicemen mingling behind; note also the masked headlights and white-painted wingtips. Following the end of hostilities all four three-axle Tigers returned to their former use at Eastbourne, surviving until 1952. *W. J. Haynes / Southdown Enthusiasts' Club*

7. THE LONGEST DAY

When it came to day trips from Brighton there was no doubt that the longest was by service 122 to Gravesend. The 122 was introduced in 1948 and was some 65 miles in length, with a journey time of a little over four hours. If there is one thing that's been learned in writing these books it's not to make definitive statements, on the basis that someone will always prove you wrong! I shall therefore refrain from declaring that it was the longest route in the country, but it certainly came close.

The 119 between Brighton and Tunbridge Wells had been operating since before the war and was worked jointly by Southdown and Maidstone & District. The 122, also jointly worked, increased the frequency between these towns to 30 minutes, for the two services followed roughly the same route, although there were one or two diversions.

Initially Southdown operated the service with rebodied Leyland TDs, while Maidstone & District used Bristol K6As, many of which were Utilities also rebodied; not all, however, for some had been built in 1949, and I recall being fascinated by their 'KKK' registrations. Having lived not far from Gravesend before moving to Brighton, we made the journey quite often by car to visit relatives, and I remember returning from Gravesend one night in thick fog of the kind we no longer seem to get. This was a real 'pea-souper', and my father was struggling to see the road ahead when suddenly, looming out of the gloom like a lighthouse, there appeared the rear of a K6A on the 122, which he duly followed all the way to Brighton. What a journey that was!

In the early 'Fifties Southdown introduced all-Leyland PD2/12s on the service, M&D doing likewise. From the late 'Fifties Southdown's superb East Lancs-bodied PD2s took over, and these would be the regular performers for many years. M&D also added some newer PD2s, with MCW Orion bodywork, and the contrast between these and Southdown's offering was quite drastic. 'Beauty and the beast' doesn't begin to describe it, and as far as comfort was concerned … well, suffice it to say that there was no comparison.

In later years Maidstone & District would sometimes provide an AEC Regent V with handsome Park Royal bodywork not dissimilar to that on Southdown's Guys, but, again, the interior finish and standard of comfort on the latter was vastly superior. M&D was also the first to put single-deckers onto the two routes, using AEC Reliances and even the occasional Leyland Panther. Southdown soon followed suit with

Leyland Leopards, but it was not long before the 122 was withdrawn, leaving the 119 to continue alone between Tunbridge Wells and Brighton. Over the years this route has been given numbers and for a while even a name, becoming the 'Regency Route'. As service 29 it still runs today, with frequency increased to 30 minutes and most journeys worked by Brighton & Hove.

The 119 and 122 left Brighton via the Lewes Road, beneath trolleybus wires which supplied power not only for trolleybuses on service 48 to Preston Barracks but also for those running to and from the Brighton Corporation depot. This was situated a little way to the north of the Lewes Road railway viaduct, which carried the Kemp Town branch line. The branch and viaduct are long gone, as are the trolleybus wires, but the depot survives; having housed trams and trolleybuses and served latterly as the home of Brighton Blue Bus (as the municipal operation became known), it remains in use with Brighton & Hove.

Travelling along the Lewes Road immediately after trolleybus abandonment one could experience that strange sensation caused by two familiar sights combining to form the unfamiliar. The phenomenon was brought about by the sight of Leyland TD5s — which had often trundled up and down the Lewes Road in Southdown apple green and cream — in *red* and cream, four of this type having been bought by Brighton Corporation as a stopgap pending the arrival of new Leyland PD2s. They never ventured from the flat service 48, and when their drivers refused to continue driving them they were quietly disposed of; two would end up in the West of England Transport Collection at Winkleigh in Devon, although they remain unrestored and face an uncertain future.

Before the introduction in 1961 of the Brighton Area Transport Services agreement Southdown charged higher fares within the Brighton area, to protect BH&D and the Corporation. Not only that; in some places — notably along the Lewes Road — its services even used separate bus stops. Nevertheless, Southdown did operate a number of local services in Brighton, mainly in the Lewes Road area, beyond the terminus of the 48, where the company had been quick to serve the growing estates of Moulsecoomb, Bevendean and Coldean which fell outside the terms of the existing (1939) agreement. These services were originally all numbered 13 with a variety of suffix letters, but the

East Moulsecoomb and Bevendean services were eventually re-numbered 109, 110 and 111. For many years these routes were operated almost exclusively by utility Guys, later being taken over by Leyland PD1s, Northern Counties-bodied Guy Arab IIIs and all-Leyland PD2/1s. When, in 1959, Brighton received its first 'Queen Mary' PD3s, they were allocated to these local services.

Returning to the 119 and 122, these continued via Lewes and Uckfield to Crowborough, where they made contact with M&D's 'own' services. In the early postwar years Crowborough had been home to another of the rare independents, in this case Beacon Motor Services. Southdown gained control of its stage-carriage services in 1949, and the company was totally absorbed in 1954. The name lived on, however, for Southdown's one-centre coach holidays were christened 'Beacon Tours'.

The 119 terminated at Tunbridge Wells, which was very much Maidstone & District territory. The allocation represented a cross-section of the M&D fleet, both single- and double-deck, and from around 1960 this was particularly interesting to us Brightonians in that one could observe rear-engined double-deckers some 10 years before such buses made their debut in Brighton. M&D was a very early user of the Leyland Atlantean and, along with the normal highbridge type,

had some of the original low-height variants with sunken gangway at the rear of the upper deck; these were numbered in M&D's 'DL' lowbridge series. Although Atlanteans were allocated to Tunbridge Wells, they very rarely appeared on the 119/122; in fact I recall only one such instance, but there were probably others.

Also to be seen in Tunbridge Wells were London Transport vehicles, in the shape of Green Line coaches on service 704 to London and Windsor; LT even had a garage in the town especially for these vehicles. RFs had replaced the elegant 10T10s in the early 'Fifties, but in the 'Sixties the route was double-decked, receiving sleek RCLs, these representing what in terms of comfort was surely the ultimate Routemaster.

One independent to run into 'the Wells' was Warren of Ticehurst, which operated a shoppers' service, latterly on Fridays only, from Burwash. Warren operated an interesting fleet in which was a collection of Commer Avengers with various makes of bodywork, including Strachans and Yeates, and a number of Dennis Lancets, including three underfloor-engined models with Duple Ambassador bodies, purchased from East Kent. However, the vehicle normally used on the Tunbridge Wells service was a lowly Bedford OB, albeit painted in Warren's striking livery of yellow and Prussian blue. The Bedford was sold when the service was withdrawn in 1965.

Above: One of the main corridors out of Brighton is the Lewes Road, along which Southdown buses would travel to Tunbridge Wells, Hawkhurst and (via the inland 25 route) Eastbourne. As far as Preston Barracks they would be duplicated by Brighton Corporation vehicles. Returning to the Old Steine on route 26 from Hollingbury, Corporation AEC/Weymann trolleybus 38 (FUF 38) swings round The Level, at the bottom of Ditchling Road. The helmet-less scooter rider would be considered reckless today! *John Bishop*

70

Left: Having left the bus station at Uckfield southbound services were faced with the steep ascent of the High Street, as apparent from this view of Maidstone & District all-Leyland PD2 DH391 (NKT 887) heading for Brighton in the summer of 1966. In pursuit are an interesting crop of contemporary cars; immediately behind the bus is a Ford Anglia 105E, while further back, being overtaken by a Rover 90, are a Mini and a Bedford Dormobile. *Dave Brown*

Above: Arguably Southdown's most handsome Leyland Titan PD2 double-deckers were the final batch of East Lancs-bodied examples dating from 1957. Combine this with the beautiful Ashdown Forest in the Sussex Weald and one is close to Heaven! In this tranquil scene, recorded in 1967, No 805 (RUF 205) heads south towards Uckfield with a light load over the 'forest' on the long 122 route from Gravesend to Brighton. *Dave Brown*

71

Right: In 1954 Southdown took delivery of its first Leyland Tiger Cubs, with bodywork by Nudd Bros & Lockyer (part of the Duple group). When new these buses had dark-green roofs, which attractive feature was later abandoned. Nevertheless, freshly repainted 627 (MUF 627) still looked well when photographed in Crowborough High Street while on local route 116 to Jarvis Brook in the 1960s. *Malcolm Keeping*

Right: On the edge of the company's territory Southdown buses would encounter those of various operators, and in some eyes none was better than fellow BET subsidiary Maidstone & District. Southdown services met up with M&D's at both East Grinstead and Tunbridge Wells, which towns were linked by M&D route 91, the latter company's SO30 (HKL 840), a Beadle-bodied AEC Regal II of 1947, being seen in Tunbridge Wells. Three of this batch were converted to open-top to undertake tours of Hastings and thankfully survive in preservation. *W. J. Haynes / Southdown Enthusiasts' Club*

Left: On a bright day in June 1969, with the sunshine showing off its splendid, simple but effective livery of green with cream waistband, London Transport RT599 (HLX 416) on route 423 pauses in the Kent village of Wrotham, where a connection could be made with the joint Southdown/M&D 122. Note the green driver's uniform, completing the professional appearance and emphasising the independence of the Country Area. Seldom seen today is the shop or business name painted on the side of the building. *Dave Brown*

Continuing northwards, the 122 reached Tonbridge. Again, this was very much Maidstone & District land, but it also served as the terminus for three London Transport Country Area routes — the 402 from Bromley, the 403 from Croydon and the 454 from Chipstead. All were worked by RTs. The 402 survives today; extended to Tunbridge Wells, it is operated by Arriva Kent & Sussex as successor to Maidstone & District, using special red-liveried DAFs.

Although longer than the 31, the 122 was a much more scenic route, and this was particularly true of the section between Tonbridge and Wrotham, where hedges would sometimes brush against both sides of the bus and the scenery would include the traditional Kent oast houses. Wrotham was another meeting place with LT, notably Green Line route 709 and, for a while, the circuitous 423 from Dartford and Longfield.

And so to Gravesend. Although very much an outpost of the Southdown empire, this too was a 'border' town, where London Transport met M&D. The main LT route was the 480 from Dartford and Erith, which during the war years had been my local route, operated by STLs, often of the forward-entrance variety. These had given way in the 'Fifties to the all-conquering RT, but in the 'Sixties the 480 was another of the Country routes to receive RMLs. Three Green Line routes reached Gravesend, these being the 701 from Ascot, the 702 from Sunningdale and the orbital 725 from Windsor via Croydon; all were RF-operated.

Maidstone & District's services in Gravesend ran mainly to and from the Medway Towns, the vehicles being the usual mix of Bristols and Leylands. There was always a chance, however, that one of the ex-Chatham & District Guys might put in an appearance — a rarity indeed for those of us from the southern end of the system, for these rarely ventured far from the Medway. There was also one occasion when, looking at a prewar Leyland TD, I felt a twinge of excitement as my eye fell on its fleet number — DH1.

Above: Given Southdown's association with the South Coast it is sometimes hard to imagine contact with London Transport's Country Area. However, travelling through Kent, route 122 would encounter LT's 454 in Tonbridge High Street. One is not quite sure which was more privileged — Southdown's PD2s or London's RTs, such as RT4505 (OLD 725), seen near Sevenoaks Weald *en route* for Tonbridge in June 1969. No doubt the debate could rage indefinitely, so just savour this superb tranquil scene! *Dave Brown*

Right: Parking on the pavement is nothing new, as demonstrated by the gleaming Ford Corsair in this June 1969 view of Brighton-bound 807 (RUF 207), an East Lancs-bodied Leyland PD2, on route 122 in Wrotham. Note that whilst the 'ultimate' blind is set for Brighton, the 'via' screen has been left with Kent locations and will be reset at Tunbridge Wells to cater for Sussex locations. *Dave Brown*

8. INTO THE POOL

Six Southdown 'country' services left Brighton via the Lewes Road. All were hourly, giving a combined 10-minute frequency between Brighton and Lewes. Three were normally worked by Park Royal-bodied Guy Arab IVs, these being the 16 to Golden Cross (where it connected with the 92 to Hailsham), the 20 to Chailey and the 25 to Eastbourne via Lewes and Polegate. The 119 and 122 we know from the previous chapter, while the sixth was the 18 to Hawkhurst. Like the 119 and 122 this was operated jointly with Maidstone & District and was a 'Leyland route'. Memory suggests that Southdown's Leyland-bodied PD2/12s predominated with M&D providing its equivalent, although in later days M&D's AEC Regent Vs became a common sight; eventually, like most others, the service succumbed to the 36ft single-decker before being withdrawn completely.

The six services all ran along the main A27 through Falmer to Lewes.

Besides the castle and Anne of Cleeves' house Lewes is famous for its steep hills and narrow streets. Over the years the town has been subjected to pedestrianisation and one-way traffic schemes, and it is now hard to believe that double-deckers once passed each other where today there seems barely room for one. Buses entering the town from Brighton passed the Prison and negotiated the 'bottleneck' before dropping down steep School Hill to the bus station. Like those at Chichester and Haywards Heath, the bus station had been built in the mid-'Fifties. Along with a waiting room, an enquiry office, staff accommodation and a buffet there was a garage (for 19 buses) and simple maintenance facilities. With the projected takeover by Brighton & Hove of most services between Brighton and Tunbridge Wells the garage was due to close in 2005, and the bus station itself faces an uncertain future.

Right: Lewes, the county town of East Sussex, was once the meeting-point for a number of Southdown services, sufficient to warrant the building of a bus station in the 1950s. Seen in the early 1970s on local route 29 to Ringmer is 113 (113 CUF), a Leyland Leopard with Marshall bodywork to BET Federation design; behind is a dual-purpose Northern Counties-bodied Leopard, 452 (NUF 452G), on route 25 from Brighton to Eastbourne. The bus station still survives, but the adjacent garage (out of shot to the left) was expected to close in September 2005 with the takeover by Brighton & Hove of most workings between Brighton, Lewes and Tunbridge Wells. *Malcolm Keeping*

Left: Views of Maidstone & District buses in the centre of Lewes are not commonplace, so it is pleasing to be able to include this view of Weymann-bodied Leyland PD2/12 DH435 (RKP 916) of 1954 opposite Lewes Crown Court on joint Southdown/M&D route 119 from Tunbridge Wells to Brighton. *W. H. R. Godwin*

From the bus station the 18 passed under the bridge that carried the Lewes–Uckfield–Tunbridge Wells railway line before crossing the River Ouse by means of the old humpback bridge. This would appear to have been an ideal spot for bus photography, but few pictures taken at this location seem to exist. The railway bridge is no more, and Cliffe High Street is partially pedestrianised, buses using Phoenix Causeway and passing Tesco's instead of the old Odeon cinema, where the 18 used to turn left before climbing Malling Hill. Leaving the A26 at Earwig Corner, the 16 and 18 finally parted company on the far side of Ringmer, the 18 continuing to Cross-in-Hand and Heathfield.

Roughly midway between Eastbourne and Tunbridge Wells, Heathfield is a small market town on the ridge of the Weald and was another of the 'border' towns where Southdown met Maidstone & District. From here Southdown's services radiated mainly to the west

and south, to Uckfield, Lewes and Eastbourne, while those of M&D spread northwards and eastwards, to Tunbridge Wells, Hawkhurst and Hastings. In 1957 the two companies decided to co-ordinate their services in an effort to improve through workings, and from then on all routes serving Heathfield (with the exception of an infrequent service to Eastbourne via Waldron) were jointly operated under a complex system of inter-working known as the 'Heathfield Cycle' or 'Heathfield Pool'.

Mention has already been made of Southdown's prowess at providing connecting services, but the Heathfield Pool was little short of masterly. From the inception of the scheme the 18 became two-hourly, the intervening journeys being undertaken by a new route 180, also two-hourly, which followed the same route as far as Heathfield before continuing via Battle to Hastings; the 'missing' journeys

between Heathfield and Hawkhurst were covered by service 190 from Eastbourne. The arrangement isn't easily explained but worked broadly as follows:

	First Hour	Second Hour
Brighton–Hawkhurst	18 through	180 to Heathfield, change to 190
Brighton–Hastings	18 to Heathfield, change to 152	180 through
Eastbourne–Hawkhurst	190 to Heathfield, change to 18	190 through
Tunbridge Wells–Eastbourne	152 to Heathfield, change to 190	191 through
Tunbridge Wells–Hastings	152 through	191 to Heathfield, change to 180

In addition, joint service 192 operated from Eastbourne to Uckfield via Heathfield and together with services 190 and 191 gave a 30-minute frequency between Eastbourne and Heathfield as well as providing further connections with the 119 and 122 at Uckfield. One of my first jobs on leaving school and joining Southdown was to allocate the mileage between the two companies; needless to say, this was not an easy task, and it is perhaps not surprising that on occasion a bus sent out on 'Pool' services would disappear for two or three days!

From Heathfield the 18 continued on to Burwash — a journey that afforded spectacular views of the Weald from the upper deck — and thence to Etchingham and Hurst Green, where it met up with M&D's 5 and 57 from Hastings to Maidstone and Gravesend respectively, joining them for the final run into Hawkhurst.

Terminus for a number of M&D services, Hawkhurst had a bus station and garage that are little changed today, although the buses are now mainly aquamarine and Cotswold stone instead of dark green and cream. Also running into Hawkhurst, albeit terminating at the town-centre shops rather than the bus station, was the service from Rye of John Dengate & Sons. Dengate was a typical small independent, whose fleet over the years contained a motley collection of vehicles including some real gems; more on these in Chapter 10. Suffice to say for now that, however interesting the fleet may have been, the vehicles usually provided for the Hawkhurst service were Bedford OBs.

Above: Operated jointly with Maidstone & District as part of the Heathfield Pool was route 18 from Brighton to Hawkhurst, about three miles over the county boundary in Kent. Although Hawkhurst is but a small town the bus station and M&D garage would not have looked out of place in a large conurbation. A pair of handsome all-Leyland PD2s — DH380/8 (NKT 876/84) — almost identical to Southdown's (701-54) take pride of place basking outside the garage in the spring sunshine of 1967. *Dave Brown*

Far right: Alternate journeys
on Southdown route 12 to
Eastbourne started from
Withdean, reaching the
town centre by way of Dyke
Road, which they shared with
local services provided by
Brighton Corporation.
Firm favourites with enthusiasts
of all ages were the latter's
superb Weymann-bodied
AEC Regent IIIs, including 92
(KCD 92), seen in Dyke Road
passing a newly painted former
tram shelter which since this
photograph was taken in the
mid-1960s has been moved
off the road, being protected
to some degree by the wall
on the right. *Malcolm Keeping*

When the 18 and its fellows turned left at the old Lewes Odeon, the 25 turned right, shortly passing Light's scrapyard at Southerham, where so many Southdown buses — not to mention all but one of Brighton Corporation's AEC trolleybuses — met their ultimate fate. It then meandered along the A27, wandering off to serve Firle Place and then on through Berwick and Selmeston. It was rather like a sleepy branch liner, never in a hurry, the Gardner 6LW of the Guy Arab throbbing away as if it would go on for ever. At Polegate Crossroads the tempo quickened a little as the bus turned southwards through Willingdon and into Eastbourne's Pevensey Road bus station.

The journey from Brighton took around an hour and a half and offered a largely rural ride through some attractive Sussex countryside. Like so many similar services it was never the same once the single-deckers took over and that popular slogan 'You see more from the top of a bus' became obsolete. As well as being a pleasant ride in itself, it formed part of a particularly enjoyable circular trip when linked with the coastal service 12.

The 12 was another of Southdown's prestige services which, together with the 31, usually received the newest vehicles. It was also the service on which Southdown tried out its demonstrators, and at various times a Leyland Olympic single-decker, a rear-engined Leyland LowLoader (precursor of the Atlantean), a Guy Wulfrunian and an Alexander-bodied Daimler Fleetline were all put through their paces on the 12 road.

The 12 was unusual amongst long-distance routes in that it didn't start from Pool Valley. Between Dyke Road and London Road in Brighton was an exclusive residential area known generally as Withdean and by Southdown as Tongdean, and which, following further housing development in the 'Fifties,' became known as West Dene! It was an area which neither Brighton, Hove & District nor Brighton Corporation had penetrated, and it was from here that alternate service 12 journeys to Eastbourne began, the remaining two journeys per hour starting from Brighton station. There were also two short-workings based on the 12 — the 12A from Withdean to Peacehaven Annexe and the 12B from Brighton station to Saltdean Mount.

Leaving Withdean, the 12 and 12A headed down Dyke Road in company with Brighton Corporation routes 51 and 52 to the Old Steine. The Dyke Road service had originally been tram route 'N' and was the

only one to be replaced by motor buses rather than trolleybuses. The 51 was a direct replacement, running via Seven Dials, Preston Circus and London Road, while the 52 served Brighton station before continuing down West Street to the seafront. From 1939 the two routes had been worked by the famous 'FUF'-registered AEC Regents with 8.8-litre engines and Weymann bodywork; in the late 'Forties these were joined by AEC Regent IIIs, again with Weymann bodies — a classic combination if ever there was one. The scales tipped somewhat in 1959, when Leyland PD2s with spartan Weymann Orion bodywork became the order of the day.

At Brighton station the Southdown services were privileged in using the access road beneath the canopy of the station forecourt, while the services of BH&D and the Corporation used the stands in the roadway outside. Leaving the station, the 12 group of services descended Queen's Road and North Street, eventually entering Pool Valley. Only eastbound journeys did so, however, westbound workings using the bus stand in Old Steine, which they shared with the local Lewes Road services.

From Pool Valley the 12 headed eastwards along Marine Parade, which road it shared for many years with BH&D service 4 (Southwick–Rottingdean), a route that in the late 1950s was worked exclusively by highbridge Bristol KSWs. Before the building of the Marina the only leisure facilities at Black Rock were an open-air swimming pool and the terminus of Volk's Electric Railway. For the bus enthusiast there was an added attraction, this being the terminus of BH&D route 44, and here one could observe that rarity, the Tilling-group trolleybus. BH&D operated 11 trolleybuses as part of the 1939 agreement between itself and Brighton Corporation. Eight were AECs, delivered in 1939 but stored during the war, and three postwar BUTs. All had Weymann bodywork and were basically similar to the Corporation's, albeit with sufficient minor differences to make identification fairly simple.

From Black Rock the 12 kept to the coast road that ran along the cliff top, passing the famous Roedean girls' school and St Dunstan's Home for the Blind before dropping down into the picturesque village of Rottingdean. From 1939 to 1961 this was the eastern boundary for BH&D and Corporation services, being the terminus for BH&D's long service 2 from Kingston Lane, the 4 from Southwick and the 7, also

from Southwick, which over the years was operated by both BH&D and the Corporation. Rottingdean was also the turning-point for the famous open-top service 17.

Following the implementation of the BATS agreement in 1961 the eastern boundary was set at Telscombe, taking BH&D and Corporation buses beyond their former terminus, and services in this part of the town were amongst the first to be rationalised. BH&D service 4 was a casualty of these changes and was replaced by a new service 55 to East Saltdean, a growing area hitherto unserved by public transport. Southdown's service 12B from Brighton station to Saltdean Mount was also replaced, the new service being numbered 39 and extended westwards to Hove station and Hove Lagoon. The service was allocated to Brighton Corporation, and regular passengers must have experienced quite a culture shock when Orion-bodied PD2s with spartan interiors, no heaters and open platforms took over from Southdown's Park Royal, Beadle- and East Lancs-bodied examples.

BRIGHTON HOVE & DISTRICT
TRANSPORT

JULY, 1957
TIMETABLE
AND MAP
6d

Right: A busy late-1950s scene in North Street, Brighton, featuring Southdown 1956 Guy Arab IV/ Park Royal 550 (PUF 650) on route 12 ahead of a Brighton, Hove & District Bristol KSW6G, 486 (LNJ 486), on the 2A to South Woodingdean, with another Southdown Guy — 544 (PUF 844) — on the 12B to Saltdean and an unidentified BH&D K type on the 3A to Whitehawk bringing up the rear. Briefly, pending the arrival of more Leylands, the Guys were regular performers on this corridor, the Gardner 6LW engine, whilst something of a 'plodder', proving capable of taking the route's steep hills in its stride. *Glyn Kraemer-Johnson collection*

Left: Route 112 was inter-worked with the 12 group of services, which operated east from Brighton towards Eastbourne; a circular serving the West Dene and Tongdean estates, it duplicated Corporation routes 51 and 52 in Dyke Road. With a full screen display and no advertisements, Northern Counties-bodied Leyland PD3 899 (2899 CD) is seen in Pool Valley soon after delivery in 1961. *John Bishop*

Right: In the 1970s all-over advertising was a source of much-needed revenue for bus companies faced with ever-diminishing passenger numbers. Southdown was no exception, as demonstrated by 'Queen Mary' Leyland PD3/ Northern Counties 263 (BUF 263C) in Rediffusion livery, bound for Newhaven on route 12C in June 1974. This scene in Brighton's Old Steine includes on the left one of the last red-liveried Corporation buses — Leyland PD2/Weymann 58 (WCD 58) — and, in the background, disappearing up St James's Street, an ex-BH&D Bristol Lodekka in Southdown green. *John Bishop*

Above: A scene at Pool Valley, Brighton, in the summer of 1967.
Taking pride of place is brand-new Leyland Titan PD3/4 368 (HCD 368E),
with Northern Counties 'panoramic' bodywork, on local route 112.
All other vehicles in view are Park Royal-bodied; on the left, Guy Arab IV
534 (PUF 634) has blinds set for route 20 to Chailey (King's Head),
while on the right, Leyland PD2/12 766 (OCD 766) prepares to depart for
Lewes on the 24. Just visible in the background is a Maidstone & District
AEC Regent V on layover between journeys on route 119 from/to
Tunbridge Wells. *Dave Brown*

Leaving the red-and-cream Brighton vehicles behind, the 12 continued through the untidy sprawl that was Peacehaven and descended into the harbour town of Newhaven — a typical small port, with cranes and derricks and a network of railway lines. During the 'Fifties steam-hauled boat trains would arrive at the Harbour station and, for a while after the end of steam, they continued behind electric locomotives until the demand disappeared. Nowadays not much more than a four-car multiple-unit is seen in the town.

Buses crossed the River Ouse by means of a swing bridge, originally hand-operated, that swung through 90° to allow ships to pass upstream — and much delay and frustration it caused. In 1974 it was replaced by a new structure, mechanically operated, which greatly reduced delays to buses and other traffic.

From Newhaven the road takes a wide inland curve to Denton and back to the coast at Bishopstone, a detour necessary to avoid the marshy land in between that the railway line crosses on an embankment. The stretch between Bishopstone and Seaford, being on the eastern side of Seaford Bay, receives the full force of the southwesterly gales, and it is not that uncommon for double-deckers to be replaced by singles when the winds become severe.

Seaford was the terminus of the 98 from Hailsham and the 126 from Eastbourne, both via Alfriston. Both were single-deck routes, graduating from 1400s through Beadle rebuilds to Leyland Tiger Cubs and, in the case of the 126, Leyland Nationals and Optare Solos, for it still runs today as an East Sussex County Council-supported service. The 98 has long since disappeared, the number being given to the inland route from Eastbourne to Hastings, but a surviving bus stop in Alfriston serves as a reminder.

The journey from Seaford to Eastbourne was — indeed, is — particularly scenic. Crossing the narrow Exceat Bridge and passing the entrance to the Seven Sisters Country Park, buses climb steeply, giving wonderful views across the Cuckmere estuary — a textbook example of a meandering river. The road continues to climb, running beside Friston Forest until it reaches a level not far removed from that of Beachy Head.

From here the 12 would begin to descend East Dean Road with views across the town of Eastbourne and as far as Hastings. Coasting down the hill was one thing; climbing it in a PD1 was quite a different kettle of fish, but then PD1s worked the route only briefly, even though a representation of such a vehicle on route 12 adorned the front of Southdown's timetable for many years.

Before World War 2, perhaps strangely for such an important route, the 12 was operated by single-deckers — 1400-class Leyland Tiger TS7s in an attractive livery of apple green with cream waistband and roof; the dark-green roof was a wartime innovation that remained after hostilities had ceased. Utility Guys took over when the route was double-decked, and PD1s did indeed work the route for a while when new. In 1948 the route was equipped with new all-Leyland PD2/1s, and these remained the mainstay of the service for many years until superseded by PD2/12s with various makes of body, these in turn eventually giving way to the inevitable 'Queen Marys'. There was something of a hiccup in the Leyland ancestry in 1956, when brand-new Park Royal-bodied Guy Arab IVs were used, but their stay was comparatively short.

Above: This shot, taken in Newhaven in November 1974, breaks all the rules of bus photography but is included for its historic importance, this being the first week of operation of the new swing bridge; as an added bonus we have Southdown 'Queen Mary' Leyland PD3 298 (FCD 298D), with NBC-style fleetname, bound for Brighton on route 12c. The new bridge replaced the hand-operated bridge (out of view to the right) used hitherto and significantly reduced delays on the A259 coast road between Brighton and Eastbourne.
John Bishop

As the 12 dropped down East Dean Road into Church Street one caught one's first glimpse of an Eastbourne Corporation double-decker. Blue was not a common colour for buses in the South East, and at first sight that of Eastbourne was quite startling to those of us accustomed to the reds and greens of Brighton and Southdown. The blue was a deep, rich colour set off by primrose window surrounds and a white roof. Southdown's cream is sometimes referred to as 'primrose', but Eastbourne's was a rich lemon colour. Moreover it swept down over the front mudguard, leaving the front dash and bonnet-top in the same striking colour. Advertisements were also unusual in being painted directly onto the bus in the same yellow colour, with no background.

Eastbourne had been very much a Leyland stronghold before World War 2 and carried on the tradition in 1946 by taking a batch of Leyland PD1s that started what would be a long association with East Lancashire Coachbuilders; nevertheless, there followed half a dozen AEC Regents, one Regent II and five Regent IIIs, all with bodywork by Weymann. In 1948/9, however, came Leyland PD2/1s, AEC Regent IIIs and Crossley DD42/5s, all with similar East Lancs bodies.

The AEC period began in earnest in 1951 with a batch of extremely handsome AEC Regent IIIs bodied by Bruce Coachworks of Cardiff. AEC Regent Vs were the order of the day between 1956 and 1963, and these were followed by a reversion to Leyland, in the form of 15 PD2A/30s with St Helens fronts; all were bodied by East Lancs. The PD2s turned out to be the last front-engined double-deckers bought new and the last buses delivered in the traditional blue, primrose and white, for in 1969 it was decided to adopt a bland livery of cream with a single

Right: In 1964/5 Southdown replaced its Guy Arab open-toppers with Leyland Titan PD3s with convertible Northern Counties bodywork. One of the latter, 426 (BUF 426C), is seen at the eastern end of Royal Parade, Eastbourne, on the lengthy and circuitous 197 route, which not only took in Beachy Head but also reached Birling Gap before heading back into town along the main A259 road. Prior to 1969 the stretch of road in the background was occupied by the Eastbourne Miniature Tramway. *John Bishop*

Right: Eastbourne's purchasing policy had shown a preference for Leyland and AEC products, so it came as quite a surprise when, in the late 1960s, the Daimler Roadliner (along with the Leyland Panther) was chosen to fulfil the Corporation's newly identified single-deck requirements. Pictured in Cornfield Road in 1973, sleek-looking Roadliner/East Lancs 90 (EJK 890F) would have a comparatively short life on account of the type's reliability problems. *John Bishop*

blue band at lower-deck waist level, and some of the magic went out of the Eastbourne fleet. The Borough Council then had a brief, somewhat painful affair with single-deckers, taking Daimler Roadliners and Leyland Panthers, before turning to the Atlantean.

Like most seaside resorts Eastbourne had its open-top services, in this case worked by both Southdown and Eastbourne Corporation. A landmark as famous as Beachy Head obviously became the prime destination for an open-top service, but this was strictly Southdown territory, Corporation buses having to turn at the foot of the famous headland. Two services were operated, the 97 to Beachy Head and the 197 to Beachy Head and Birling Gap. Before the war double-deckers were banned from the Beachy Head route, and Southdown had used six-wheel Leyland Tiger TS6T and TS7T single-deckers. In 1952 the restriction on double-deckers was lifted, and Beachy Head resounded to the throb of the Gardner 6LWs fitted to the utility Guys converted by the company to open-top. In the 'Sixties these were replaced by Northern Counties-bodied PD3s with detachable roofs. Eastbourne Corporation operated a variety of open-toppers, ranging from all-Leyland TD2s, TD5s and TD6s through East Lancs-bodied PD1s to a Leyland PD2A/30, while some of the AEC Regent Vs, with full-drop windows (rather like those on a car) and translucent roofs, were used on sightseeing services.

Quite a stir was caused in Eastbourne in 1950 when Southdown took delivery of car 700 (KUF 700). A Leyland PD2/12 fitted with a full-fronted Northern Counties body to full coach specification, it bore a slight resemblance to Ribble's 'White Ladies' but gave more than a hint of what was to come in the shape of the 'Queen Mary' PD3s. Put to work on the Eastbourne–London express service, it proved unpopular with crews and passengers alike; it was about a ton overweight, which made its performance extremely sluggish, and rolled so much that even the lower-deck passengers felt ill! Eventually it was transferred to Bognor Regis, where it eked out its days on private-hire and school duties.

Above: Nestling at the foot of the South Downs, Eastbourne prides itself as being the suntrap of the South, and both Southdown and Eastbourne Corporation operated open-top buses. This view, recorded in the summer of 1966, features the latter's 13 (JK 9111), a 1946 Leyland PD1 with East Lancs body converted in 1961/2, alongside an AEC Regent V. The smartly turned-out Corporation employees permit comparison of summer and standard uniforms. *Dave Brown*

Two routes led from Eastbourne to Hastings, both worked jointly with Maidstone & District. The first of these was the 15, which started its journey by heading northwards through Willingdon and Polegate to the small market town of Hailsham. There it stopped at the bus office in the High Street — another thoroughfare (long since made one-way) in which it is now difficult to imagine buses passing. Most towns and villages of any consequence had a bus office or an agent, the latter usually a newsagent or general stores, where one could deposit parcels for carriage by bus; they would be collected by the conductor and dropped off at the office or agent in the required town for collection by the recipient. It was a system that worked well and was very often quicker than the Royal Mail.

Hailsham was served by around a dozen services including the joint routes from Eastbourne to Heathfield and beyond and the 92 to East Grinstead; the others were mainly local rural services like the 98 to Alfriston and the 100 and 101 to Herstmonceux and Bodle Street Green.

The 15 itself continued to Herstmonceux, then home to the Royal Greenwich Observatory, before turning south through Ninfield and Sidley to Bexhill, where it met up with the other Eastbourne–Hastings service. This was the 99, which took the coast road out of Eastbourne. On the outskirts of the town, in an area of the coastal strip known as the Crumbles, was the MET, or Modern Electric Tramway. Opened in 1954, this was a 2ft-gauge tramway that ran from Prince's Park to the Crumbles — a distance of two thirds of a mile. In addition, a one-third-scale model of a London General B-type bus toured the town advertising the tramway. Applications to extend the operation were repeatedly rejected by the Borough Council, as a result of which the tramway closed in 1969 and moved to a new site at Seaton in Devon, where it not only survives but has become a thriving tourist attraction. What a loss for Eastbourne!

The 99 continued through Pevensey and Little Common until it too arrived at Bexhill. The edge of Maidstone & District territory, this was where, in the 'Fifties, the bus traveller from the west would first catch sight of a trolleybus in M&D green and cream. Hastings Tramways had abandoned its trams in 1928, replacing them with a fleet of six-wheel open-top double-deck and six-wheel centre-entrance single-deck Guy trolleybuses. Single-deck trolleybuses weren't that common anywhere,

and in the South East they were unique to Hastings. Maidstone & District acquired the undertaking in 1935, trolleybuses being painted in M&D livery but with Hastings Tramways fleetnames. There are memories of the single-deckers in service, but these are vague. Certainly by the mid-'Fifties all save one of the Guys had gone, replaced by more modern two-axle AECs and Sunbeams with Park Royal and Weymann bodies.

The motor-bus fleet was equally interesting. M&D had been a great devotee of Bristol, continuing to favour the marque until it was no longer available to non-Tilling-group companies, and in addition to the K6A double-deckers, both utility and postwar, that were to be seen throughout the company's area, there were some very attractive single-deckers in the form of ECW-bodied L6As and LL5Gs, which were a common sight in Hastings. Again, open-toppers were operated, and originally these were Leyland Titan TD5s with purpose-built open-top bodywork by Weymann. These were later replaced by AEC Regal single-deckers converted to open-top configuration by the company, together with 'Happy Harold', the sole surviving Guy double-deck trolleybus, which had been fitted with a Commer TS3 two-stroke diesel engine emitting a sound that couldn't be less like a trolleybus and which survives in preservation to this day.

The trolleybuses were absorbed completely into the M&D fleet in 1957, having Maidstone & District fleetnames applied, and two years later were withdrawn, being replaced by Leyland Atlanteans. Maidstone & District was one of the earliest users of the Atlantean, and these huge, ugly buses were very much a novelty to those of us from areas where the front-engined double-decker was to reign supreme for a further 10 years. Funny, though, how those Atlanteans no longer look either huge or ugly.

Having passed through St Leonard's, both the 15 and the 99 terminated in Wellington Square, Hastings. The square sloped steeply, and parked buses had chocks placed beneath the wheels to prevent them from rolling forward.

Wellington Square was also the terminus for three services — from Rye, Fairlight and Pett Level — operated by the East Kent Road Car Co, its crimson-and-ivory AEC Reliances adding a splash of colour to the greens of Southdown and M&D. Eventually, following

Above: Southdown buses reached Hastings on two joint routes (15 and 99) and upon arriving at their destination would (until 1959) pass under the wires of the town's Maidstone & District trolleybuses. Representing an earlier generation, however, is this GUY BTX single-decker, which for many years served as a temporary waiting room and booking office; one wonders how many intending coach passengers knew that they were waiting in an old trolleybus! Thankfully this vehicle is now preserved in Hastings, but the coach station has given way to a shopping precinct. This view dates from the very early 1970s, when an excursion to Brighton cost a mere 8s — 40p in today's currency!
John Bishop

Right: Heading east on routes 15 and 99, shared with Maidstone & District, Southdown buses would first encounter Hastings trolleybuses at Bexhill. Seen with full M&D fleetnames is 1940 AEC/Weymann 15 (BDY 790); today controlled by a complex system of traffic lights, the junction of The Ridge and Rye Road in Ore Village, Hastings, was quiet enough for trolleybuses to turn when this photograph was taken in the late 1950s. The trolleybuses would finally be withdrawn in 1959.
Lyndon Rowe / Southdown Enthusiasts' Club

Left: The new order at Hastings. Seen in Silverhill in 1959 when brand-new, its paint barely dry, is Maidstone & District Leyland Atlantean/Metro-Cammell DH499 (499 DKT). The trolleybuses have gone, and the wiring above is beginning to sag prior to removal.
John Bishop

a reallocation of services, these routes were passed to Maidstone & District, following which the only East Kent vehicles to be seen in the town were Reliances on the South Coast Express service to Bournemouth and beyond.

One further operator to be seen in Wellington Square was the independent John Dengate & Son of Beckley, near Rye. As well as his Hawkhurst service Dengate operated a route from Northiam to Hastings using mainly Bedford OBs, some having bus bodies by Mulliner as a change from the usual Duple Vista coach body. Later on one would see Bedford SBs and, towards the end, a couple of Saro-bodied Tiger Cubs bought from East Midland. Over the years Dengate operated a fascinating selection of second-hand double-deckers, including ex-

Southdown TDs and an all-Leyland PD2/1, a Willowbrook-bodied Crossley new to Delaine of Bourne and an ex-London RT; these were used mainly on schools contracts but would occasionally appear on stage services on Saturdays.

When Wellington Square was about to be redeveloped Southdown and M&D services were moved to parking places in other parts of the town. Dengate alone was allowed to remain in the square, and his bus stop eventually turned out to be right outside a brand-new Tesco store, something he thought might boost his patronage. However, it would have taken more than that to save the company, and in 1967 the services were taken over by Davies of Rye, which bought two new Ford Thames service buses with Duple Midland bodies for the purpose.

Right: Based in the East Sussex village of Beckley, near Rye, J. Dengate & Sons was a small independent which, like many such operators, ran Bedford OB-type buses, represented here by Mulliner-bodied 16 (CDY 294). Such operators always seemed to employ 'characters', typified by the smiling driver guiding his vehicle to its terminus in Wellington Square, Hastings; note how the photographer has angled his lens to compensate for the steep gradient. Dengate would be taken over by Maidstone & District in May 1974.
D. A. Jones / London Trolleybus Preservation Society

Right: The Hastings terminus for Southdown services 15 and 99 was Wellington Square, where buses parked on a steep slope. This late-1950s view features a varied selection from the Maidstone & District fleet, comprising Harrington-bodied AEC Reliance S246 (246 BKM), Weymann-rebodied Bristol K6A DH126 (HKE 227) and AEC Regent V/ Park Royal DH481 (VKR 473); on the left is Beadle-AEC rebuild SO98 (NKT 957), downgraded to bus status from coach CO229.
The Omnibus Society

Above: In Hastings Southdown buses encountered not only Maidstone & District vehicles but also those of the East Kent Road Car Co, which operated to the picturesque town of Rye. One such would have been LJG 305, a Weymann-bodied AEC Reliance dating from 1956, seen *c*1972 in the centre of Hastings; the seafront is in the background, while the clock tower is just out of view on the left. Under forthcoming reorganisation the handful of East Kent services in this area would pass to Maidstone & District, red and cream giving way to M&D's dark green and cream and, ultimately, NBC leaf green. *Ray Glover*

EPILOGUE

Right: Still *in situ* today, a reminder of Southdown days of yore, is this battered bus-stop flag in Alfriston, East Sussex. Route 98 has long since gone, whilst the 126 has been truncated under various service revisions introduced by East Sussex County Council. *John Bishop*

This, then, was the once-great Southdown empire, stretching for almost a hundred miles along the South Coast from Hastings to Warsash and spreading 65 miles inland to Gravesend at its northernmost point. Southdown emerged from the doldrums of the National Bus Company as a private company, using a variation of its traditional apple-green and cream livery, but was eventually bought by Stagecoach. Maidstone & District's Hastings operations had been established as a separate company, Hastings & District, and this too became part of Stagecoach, as indeed did the greater part of the erstwhile Aldershot & District. City of Portsmouth and Provincial have become part of FirstGroup, while Maidstone & District is now Arriva Kent & Sussex.

Some of the services explored in this book still operate today. The old 31 route still runs between Brighton and Portsmouth as service 700, whilst the Brighton–Eastbourne service, now operated entirely by Brighton & Hove, not only maintains a 15-minute frequency but has recently had its old route number, 12, restored. As already mentioned, the former 119 between Brighton and Tunbridge Wells, now shared by Brighton & Hove and Arriva, runs on a 30-minute headway as service 29, whilst the Brighton–Horsham service has also been given back its old route number of 17. The Worthing–Horsham and Brighton–Crawley services are now in the hands of Metrobus, and the Eastbourne–Tunbridge Wells service, fairly recently reinstated, is worked by Eastbourne Buses. It is still possible to travel over the old 22 route from Brighton to Petersfield, but this now involves four different buses operated by three different companies.

However, in today's deregulated industry services and operators are changing constantly, so how long these routes will continue in their present form is anyone's guess.

The more rural and local services in such places as Lewes, Haywards Heath and Arundel are now mainly supported by county councils and are operated by a multitude of independent operators. Yes, the South East now has its fair share of independents, although the Dennis Dart and Optare Solo have replaced that much-loved workhorse, the Bedford OB.

As for the Heathfield Cycle . . . well, if you don't have a car and want to travel around the Heathfield/Hawkhurst area, a cycle is probably what you'll need!